VIỆT-NAM CỘNG-HÒA
BẢN-ĐỒ HÀNH-CHÁNH
TỶ · LỆ 1: 2.000.000

NHA ĐỊA-DƯ QUỐC-GIA phát-hành lần thứ nhất 1969

Ấn-hành tháng 10 · 1969

Praise for *They Are All My Family*

"In the chaos of a frenzied war, in the mounting gyre of fear, brutality, and cowardice, one man steps forward to offer 106 terrified souls safe passage from the hellfire. What human impulse—what valor, grit, and grace—led John Riordan to countermand his orders, risk personal danger, and set himself on a perilous course to save lives in the last anarchic days of the Vietnam War? *They Are All My Family* is a thrilling account of a young banker who had every opportunity to do exactly what his country was doing—cut his losses and run—and yet he did the very opposite. Told with gripping detail, a white-knuckle sense of urgency, and, above all, a very large heart, this is a story that recalls *Schindler's List* or *The Pianist* or *The Siege of Krishnapur*. It is a triumphant tale."

—Marie Arana, author of
Bolívar: American Liberator and *American Chica*

THEY ARE ALL MY FAMILY

THEY ARE ALL MY FAMILY

A DARING RESCUE IN
THE CHAOS *of* SAIGON'S FALL

JOHN P. RIORDAN
with MONIQUE BRINSON DEMERY

PublicAffairs
New York

Published in the United States by PublicAffairs™, a Member of the Perseus Books Group
All rights reserved.
Printed in the United States of America.

PublicAffairs books are available at special discounts for bulk purchases in the U.S. by corporations, institutions, and other organizations. For more information, please contact the Special Markets Department at the Perseus Books Group, 2300 Chestnut Street, Suite 200, Philadelphia, PA 19103, call (800) 810-4145, ext. 5000, or e-mail special.markets@perseusbooks.com.

The map of Saigon, April 1975, on p. viii is based on maps dating back to 1969 and includes names and locations from the author's memories.

Library of Congress Cataloging-in-Publication Data
Riordan, John P., author.
    They are all my family : a daring rescue in the chaos of Saigon's fall / John P. Riordan with Monique Brinson Demery. -- First edition.
        pages cm
    Includes bibliographical references and index.
    ISBN 978-1-61039-503-8 (hardcover) — ISBN 978-1-61039-504-5 (e-book) 1. Vietnam War, 1961–1975—Vietnam–Ho Chi Minh City. 2. Humanitarian assistance, American—Vietnam—Ho Chi Minh City—History. 3. Vietnam War, 1961–1975—Personal narratives, American.
4. Refugees—Vietnam—Ho Chi Minh City—History. 5. Ho Chi Minh City (Vietnam)—History.
I. Demery, Monique Brinson, 1976– author. II. Title.

DS559.9.S24R56 2015
959.704'3095977—dc23

2014049615

First Edition

10 9 8 7 6 5 4 3 2 1

This book is dedicated to the memory of my loving and kind parents,
William Joseph Riordan and Rosemary Murphy Riordan,
for their gentle care, saintly patience, and guidance.
Not only did they give me the greatest gift of all, life itself,
but they taught me the importance of family.

CONTENTS

Photo section appears between pages 105 and 106.

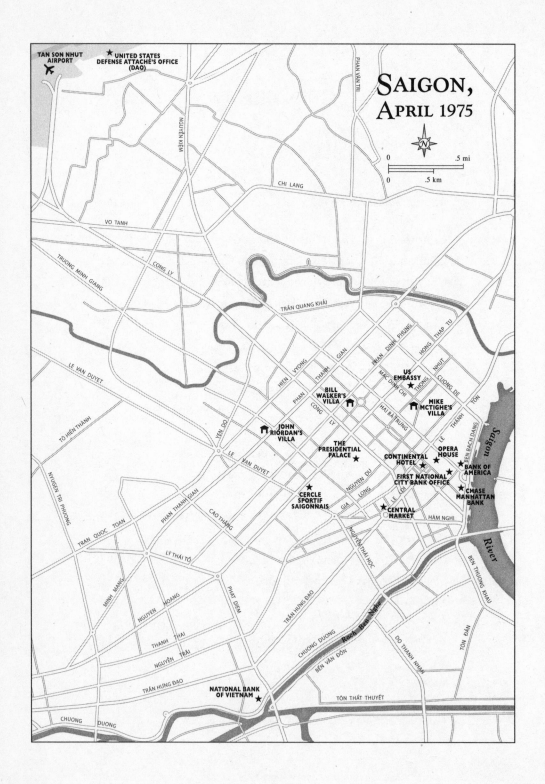

SAIGON, APRIL 1975

TAN SON NHUT AIRPORT

UNITED STATES DEFENSE ATTACHE'S OFFICE (DAO)

0 .5 mi

0 .5 km

PHAN VĂN TRI

NGUYEN KIEM

CHI LANG

VO TANH

TRUONG MINH GIANG

CONG LY

TRẦN QUANG KHẢI

LE VAN DUYET

HIEN VUONG

THANH GIAN

PHAN ĐINH PHÙNG

HONG THAP TU

NHUT

CUONG DE

US EMBASSY

MAC DINH CHI

THONG

BILL WALKER'S VILLA

PHAN

CONG LY

HAI BA TRUNG

MIKE MCTIGHE'S VILLA

LE THANH

TON

TO HIEN THANH

YEN DO

JOHN RIORDAN'S VILLA

LE VAN DUYET

THE PRESIDENTIAL PALACE

NGUYEN DU

CONTINENTAL HOTEL

OPERA HOUSE

BEN BACH DANG

Saigon

NGUYEN TRI PHUONG

GIA LONG

FIRST NATIONAL CITY BANK OFFICE

BANK OF AMERICA

TRAN QUOC TOAN

CERCLE SPORTIF SAIGONNAIS

LE LOI

CHASE MANHATTAN BANK

MINH MANG

CAO THANG

PHAN THANH GIAN

CENTRAL MARKET

HAM NGHI

River

NGUYEN HOANG

LY THAI TO

NGUYEN THAI HOC

THANH THAI

PHAT DIEM

TRẦN HƯNG ĐẠO

BEN THUONG KHAU

NGUYEN TRAI

CHUONG DUONG

BEN VAN DON

Rach Ben Nghe

DO THANH NHAN

TON DAN

TRẦN HƯNG ĐẠO

NATIONAL BANK OF VIETNAM

TÔN THẤT THUYẾT

CHUONG DUONG

CHAPTER 1

Last Flight to Saigon

"I HEARD A RUMOR," I mentioned casually to the Vietnamese ticket agent at the gate. "I hear Air Vietnam is going to end service into Saigon?"

The young woman flinched, almost imperceptibly, and recovered quickly. "That's just a lousy rumor. There's no truth to it," the young woman said firmly. She shook her long straight bangs out of her way and shot me an icy look. I glanced over my shoulder, but no one was behind me. I wasn't holding up any passengers. Hardly anyone was getting on that morning's flight from Hong Kong to Saigon. It was Friday, April 18, 1975.

The ticket agent handed me back a receipt for my one-way ticket into South Vietnam and forced a tight smile. "Don't believe any of those rumors." She smoothed the silky panels of her *ao dai*. The traditional Vietnamese dress is a knee-length tunic that the flight attendants of Air Vietnam wore in a shade of blue that matched the sky above the clouds. Despite the modesty of long sleeves, and the fact that the tunic was worn over flowing, wide-legged pants, the *ao dai* still managed to be suggestive. Long side slits showed a peek of skin above the waist, and the thin fabric hugged every curve. The ticket agent avoided my gaze and looked past me, blankly, waiting for any other passengers to board.

Except there were no more passengers. The flight was nearly empty. I chose a window seat a few rows from the front. Although I could have sworn there were at least a few others who got on the plane with me, I'll admit I was preoccupied. It was my second flight to Saigon that week. Someone told me that when they had checked the flight manifest, my name was the only one on it.

Everything else about that Friday morning flight into Saigon's Tan Son Nhut airport did seem as usual. My meal tray was distributed when the plane reached our cruising altitude. I had the ham omelet, two strips of grilled bacon, a tomato slice, and a fruit cocktail. The only reason I can recall the breakfast so clearly all these years later is because I slipped the menu into my bag as a souvenir. The Vietnamese woman drawn on the menu in orange and black ink seemed to wink at me from the cover, as if she knew exactly what I was up to.

I wasn't used to breaking rules. But that's exactly what I found myself doing by flying out of Hong Kong on a one-way ticket. It was direct defiance of my bosses at the bank. They had ordered me to stay away from Saigon, and I was heading right for it. There was not a doubt in my mind that I would be fired. There was also no doubt that it was the right thing to do. As for that lousy rumor, the one that Air Vietnam was stopping service from Hong Kong to Saigon? As it turned out, the rumor was right. My flight was the last trip the carrier would make from Hong Kong into Saigon's Tan Son Nhut airport.

The strangest feeling of calm came over me the moment the plane's wheels touched down on the tarmac. I was in Saigon on my own, under my own authority. Instead of feeling alone or scared, I felt fine. That feeling took me completely by surprise.

"John, you no longer work for the bank," I told myself, tentatively probing the thought, the way I might test a bruise. I wanted to see how bad it would feel. But it wasn't so bad at all. I seemed to have left any fears and doubts at high altitude above South Vietnam. Logically, that made no sense. Things were, by all reasonable measures, bleak. The North Vietnamese Army was approaching, and South Vietnamese cities were collapsing faster than people could leave.

I heard horror stories of fleeing refugees dropping dead of exhaustion by the side of the road. Mothers in the countryside were handing their babies off to anyone with a white face, anyone who might get their child on a boat or a plane. The capital city of Saigon and the surrounding areas were the last refuge. No South Vietnamese citizen was allowed to leave the country. Technically all they needed was an exit visa and immigration papers. But those had proved impossible for the average citizen to get. The bank had tried. My friends and colleagues at the bank would be stranded. They would be at the mercy of the Communists unless I thought of something. That was worth getting fired for.

———————————

I had no suitcase, and my carry-on was almost empty in my hands. I was hoping I wouldn't be in Saigon long enough to need much more. I had brought one fresh shirt and a toothbrush, and the souvenir menu. Light-handed as I was, I made my way easily through the airport. Things were oddly quiet in the arrival area. The immigration officer looked to be barely out of his teens and couldn't be bothered to do more than glance at my paperwork. Coming into the country was easy enough; it was getting out that was going to be the problem. My papers were in order, but I was just as glad not to have to answer any questions about why I was here on a one-way ticket or how I was leaving. I was still hoping an exit plan would come to me.

A fleet of blue-and-yellow Renault taxi cabs waited by the arrival gate, and I hailed one easily. I gave the driver the address of the bank's Saigon branch, 28–30 Nguyen Van Thinh Street, and leaned back, shifting against the springs under the seat cushion. The view out the taxi's window looked the same to me as when I had left, two weeks ago, at the beginning of April. Tiny apartments nested together like cells in a honeycomb on the edge of the city. Alleys teemed with city life and crisscrossing laundry wires. Silk pants fluttered next to sun-bleached Army uniforms. Cyclos, the traditional Vietnamese open-air carriages for one or two, were pedaled from behind by drivers on high bicycle seats. Someone had told me to expect not to see any cyclos; their drivers were said to have been banned from the city center because too many of them were feared to be Communist infil-trators. But I saw plenty. Those not in use had drivers waiting for customers, straddling their pedals, smoking and chatting as usual. They looked at ease. Market stalls were open and women in con-ical hats bobbed up and down the boulevards. I rolled down the glass and hung my elbow out the window, breathing in the sour and musty smell the city took on when it needed a good rain.

First National City Bank's Saigon branch was located in the downtown commercial area, a short walk from either city hall or the Saigon River. All the big international commercial interests had their offices in that part of town. Bank of America was across the street, and Chase Manhattan was just a block away. There were plenty of Vietnamese stores, restaurants, and small hotels, along with side-walk food vendors and mechanics repairing bikes, motorcycles, and cars. Most of the buildings were just a few stories high, though a few ambitious constructions might have reached seven or eight. The buildings were a combination of brick and concrete, painted or whitewashed various colors. The French architecture was left over from the seventy years Vietnam was a French colony. Many of the buildings would have looked at home on the boulevards of Paris but for their prominent colors—a deep yellow and white. Saigon's streets were lined with small street lights and lots of lighted neon advertising signs, but no garish glow could distract from the charm of the city. Though the bank's street was fairly sparse of greenery, the surrounding blocks had lots of old trees, often planted in parkways, which led to the city being called the "Pearl of the Orient."

It was after eleven a.m. when I pushed open the main doors to the bank. We should have been bustling that time of day, and just before a weekend. But it was quiet; there were no customers. The glass door closed behind me, leaving me alone on the polished terrazzo floor in front of the long tellers' counter. Ten pairs of eyes turned toward me.

The head teller, Chi, was the first to let out a yelp of surprise. She called to the woman next to her, who called to the woman next to her, and so on. An excited chatter circled the lobby: "Mr. Riordan is back!" I heard someone cheer. Young women who worked in the retail area of the bank beamed at me as they rushed out from their stations. Someone must have slipped upstairs because I could hear a flurry of feet suddenly thundering down. They came from the operations stations and the now-defunct marketing department on the second floor. So much for composure—I was surrounded by a cheering crowd.

"I always believed it!" Chi later told me. "You said you were coming back, and then you did. I was very happy to see you, though."

The voices and faces blurred around me. The magnitude of what I had done, and what I was about to do, was hitting me all at once. Two dozen of my colleagues were pressing around me in a tight circle.

Not everyone had had as much faith in me as Chi had. People got very emotional and cried right there on the banking floor. Others were clapping and shouting, "He's come back!" Emotions kept in check for weeks, all for the sake of the bank and of normalcy, came rushing out. A din echoed off the high ceilings and glass partitions. I was glad to see my bank colleagues too, but I didn't want to make a fuss.

Questions began to fly at me from every angle. "What do we do?" "How are we getting out of here?" I looked around at their worried and questioning faces, but I was at a loss for words.

Our bank put a big emphasis on teamwork. I had met each employee's family a few times, at the occasional holiday party or bank gathering, and I was very fond of all of them. We always had a pleasant work environment. But the truth was, outside our bank jobs, I didn't know anyone that well. We didn't socialize together unless we were entertaining clients, and in my role as assistant manager responsible for marketing for FNCB Saigon, I was mostly focused on the clients.

As I took in the faces surrounding me, I suddenly realized that my focus had changed. I might not have a job at the bank anymore, but I had the most important task of my life in front of me. The safety of my colleagues, and their families, was in my hands.

How many of them, I wondered, were thinking of their families at that moment? Lien, the senior clerk typist, had three boys and was married to a fighter pilot in the South Vietnamese Air Force. Chi had six children and was married to a high-ranking official in the military. Huy had three kids and was expecting his wife to give birth to their fourth any day.

Chuyen, the most senior Vietnamese official at the bank, had a wife and a two-and-a-half-year-old son. Chuyen had fled the Communists in North Vietnam as a young man, studied in the United States, and served in the South Vietnamese Army. His high-ranking position in our bank, itself a shining emblem of American capitalism, made him a prime target for Communist punishment. But Chuyen was calm. He picked his way through the staff until we faced each other. That finally quieted the others down. They wanted to hear what we were going to say to each other.

A smile tickled the corners of Chuyen's mouth behind his beard. I could read the relief in his face. It had been a trying few weeks. The exhaustion of it showed in circles under his eyes.

"Thank you for coming back, John. It is good to see you here." He took my outstretched hand in his. "What are the arrangements?" Chuyen asked so casually that it was almost conversational.

"Well, I don't know yet," I confessed.

Chuyen gamely nodded as if he understood. As the most senior of the local staff, he had to be strong and hopeful to inspire confidence in the rest of the employees. I didn't want anyone to be too hopeful, I realized. I didn't want to lead anyone astray.

"Before we go any further, I've got to tell you all something." I gathered myself up to my full height, just over six feet and one inch. I stood as straight as the army had taught me and looked Chuyen squarely in the eye. It was dead quiet now, and the staff was staring at me. It was time for the honest truth. "I don't think I work for FNCB anymore. I'm not a bank officer anymore."

Chuyen's face paled, and his eyebrows shot up.

He immediately grasped the magnitude of what I left unsaid. I had come back to Saigon for him and the rest of the staff, and by doing so, I had sacrificed my job. Chuyen was shocked.

I was too. I've always been the kind of guy who follows rules. I don't tend to rush into things, and I respect authority. But it sure felt good to be in Saigon. It felt good to know that I was doing the right thing and to see that my presence brought relief—and hope.

Then I had a sudden realization that stopped me cold. I hadn't considered it before, but without the bank's backing, was I still the kind of man people would follow? I looked at Chuyen. Would he, or anyone, still want to come with me? And how would I pay for any kind of escape, whether by boat or plane or helicopter, without the bank?

Chuyen seemed not to notice the sudden appearance of sweat on my upper lip. He was thinking about something intently. He absent-mindedly stroked the long hairs of his beard. Vietnamese men of a certain age and rank tend to grow these whiskers. They compel deference and respect, and when Chuyen spoke, it was quiet and slow, as if he were considering a matter of some great weight.

"When you left, didn't you, legally, officially, and fully appoint me to be the acting manager of FNCB Saigon?"

I nodded yes. When the bank had ordered me out of Saigon on April 4, I had handed the mantle to Chuyen. He had been acting as manager of the branch for two weeks. I couldn't see where Chuyen was going with this line of thinking, but he paid me no mind. Chuyen's eyes were bright now, and he had stopped pulling on his whiskers. Instead, Chuyen's words picked up steam, and he began talking through a toothy smile.

"Yes, yes, you did. You fully, legally empowered me to take acts on behalf of the bank," he said.

I was very aware that the whole bank was watching us, and I wondered where Chuyen could possibly be going with this, reasoning like Perry Mason in front of a jury.

"I hereby resign," said Chuyen with theatrical flourish. He looked up at me and stuck out his hand for me to shake again. Chuyen then pronounced over our shaking hands for the whole staff of the bank to hear: "I appoint you, John Riordan, the new acting manager of FNCB Saigon, legally, officially, and fully empowered to act on behalf of the bank. And this is to be effective immediately!"

I could have hugged Chuyen right then and there. It was brilliant. As branch manager, he had the authority, at least temporarily, to hire anyone he wanted. It seemed he had done just that. If we ever had the chance to argue it in front of the bank's top management, his maneuver might even hold some water—we did have a bank full of cheering witnesses. But that was assuming that we were going to make it out of Saigon. And that was still a very risky assumption.

CHAPTER 2

April 3, Saigon

The Call

T HE CHAIN OF EVENTS that led to my coming back to Saigon at the end of April started with a phone call. I hadn't heard the phone ring, but I looked up from my desk to see Betty Tuyet, the branch manager's secretary, standing in the door to the office with a memo pad in her hand. "That was Pan Am on the line. New York called for you."

I must have had a quizzical look on my face because she patiently explained that although the call was from our bank's Head Office in New York, it came to Pan Am's Saigon office instead of to the branch.

Betty continued. "Mr. Topping suggests that you can take it there, if you can come right down?"

Betty was younger than I was, but she had been at her job longer. In fact, Betty was the branch's very first hire in Saigon. The bank I worked for, First National City Bank of New York, wouldn't begin calling itself Citibank until later in 1975, and Citigroup still later after that, so in April we were still using the bulky acronym FNCB to refer to it.

Betty had come from American Express when its Saigon office closed down. Unlike our bank, American Express had run military

11

banking facilities, which had been very profitable. But it had no interest in trying to do business in South Vietnam after the Americans left the war. American Express openly stated its opinion that FNCB was crazy to try to make money in such a volatile climate. But Betty had come with the highest recommendations. "If you want someone to get something done in Saigon, Betty's your best bet," an American Express executive had told Bob Hudspeth, the first branch manager who set up the Saigon branch for FNCB. Bob and Betty had started FNCB's Saigon branch out of a two-room suite at the Caravelle Hotel. The manager had since moved on to a new position with a new bank somewhere else in Asia, but Betty had stayed on. Now her boss was supposed to be Mike McTighe, but since he was out of town, it was me.

"Sure, I'll take the call there," I said to Betty as I nodded and stood, casually patting the pockets of my suit jacket to make sure I had a pen and small pad of paper. It didn't occur to me to think twice about the rerouted international call. Pan Am was only a few blocks away from our office. The phone lines had always been unreliable, and I did think they seemed to be getting worse. I supposed it was one of the hazards of doing business in Saigon.

"I'll go right to my morning meeting from there. See you later, Betty," I said, following her out, and closing the door to the manager's office behind me.

I hurried down the half flight of stairs to the main level. The bank had just opened for the day; only a few customers stood in front of the long tellers' counter conducting business. One of the two Pakistani guards stationed next to the door tilted his head, acknowledging me on my way out as I headed into the rising heat of the day.

Pan Am was not one of our clients, though Lord knows, we had been trying to land that account ever since FNCB set up shop in Saigon. The airline had huge operations in Vietnam and Cambodia, all of them directed by an executive named Al Topping. I had never met Al, but he and his wife were good friends with Bill Walker, FNCB Saigon's senior operations officer, and his wife. As I walked toward Pan Am, I thought how very thoughtful it was of Al to let me know about the rerouted call. At FNCB, we all took seriously what the Head Office called "relationship banking." We were nice to people, whether they did deals with us or not; their interest was our bottom line. It was a sincere business in those days, but it was still nice to see the favor returned. I thought Pan Am might have been having its own share of phone issues; what did not occur to me was the thought that my bank's headquarters in New York might have called me out of the office and into Pan Am on purpose.

I had to cut across Tu Do Street to continue along Nguyen Van Thinh Street in order to get to Nguyen Hue Boulevard, where the Pan Am office was located. It was a three-block walk that shouldn't have been more than five minutes from our branch, but I still tried to hurry. Long distance was expensive, and I didn't want to keep waiting whoever was on the line. My undershirt was completely pasted to the small of my back by the time I pushed through the plate glass doors etched with the airline's blue globe logo.

My eyes slid past the long line of people already formed at the counter. Not even a week had passed since the evacuation of Danang, a port city 528 miles up the coast and only about an hour-long flight away from Saigon. The city had been swollen with refugees, and attempts to get them out before the Communists arrived had been a debacle. I knew only the vaguest details, since the news was censored in Saigon. Some mornings, the papers didn't have time to fix their layout after the censors had made their cuts, so visible chunks of white space dotted the pages. Only later, when I had the chance to read the article that ran in the *New York Times* on Easter Sunday, did I understand how dire the situation in Danang had actually been:

Only the fastest, the strongest and the meanest got out today on what may be the last refugee plane from Da Nang. . . .

I saw a South Vietnamese soldier kick an old woman in the face to get aboard. . . .

People fought one another and died trying to get aboard. Others fell thousands of feet to their deaths in the sea because they could no longer cling to the undercarriage.

It was a flight out of hell.[1]

Bruce Dunning's televised account of the Danang evacuation brought the horror into American living rooms for five and a half minutes on the evening news. CBS anchor Dan Rather introduced Dunning's segment with the words "Da Nang has become a Dunkirk."

The broadcast showed throngs running for the plane as it landed, and then Dunning described how it filled—almost instantly—with young Vietnamese men, some armed and "menacing." The aircraft's mission was to gather as many women and children as it could hold, but as Dunning reported, the crew counted 268 persons, among them just five women and "two or three young children." He described the scene: "We're pulling away; we're leaving people behind. People are falling off the air stairs!" The camera then captured the plane's copilot, Ed Daly, who also happened to be the president of World Airways, punching young men still trying to get onboard while the overloaded airliner was taxiing. Daly, at six thousand feet up, was pulling in one last straggler after seven others had fallen.

Danang may have been the reason why people were visibly nervous in the Pan Am office, but I didn't give them a second thought and just continued looking for Al. From what I understood, he would be hard to miss. He was six foot two and towered over his Vietnamese employees working the ticket counter. Al was also black; at the time there weren't many black American executives working in Saigon. Later there was a movie about Al and his heroic attempts to get people on a flight out of Saigon; James Earl Jones was cast as Al, a perfect fit as far as charisma and physical presence.

Al had started off as a ticket agent himself. When he showed up at JFK airport wearing a suit and tie one day instead of his standard airline uniform, he explained to his superior that he had had some trouble with the dry cleaner. Al's boss at the time had remarked, "I like you in that suit," and Al's swift promotion trajectory was launched.[2]

By 1975, Al was director of operations in Saigon, in charge of running flights in and out of Tan Son Nhut. It had been the world's second busiest airport during the war. Commercial flights carried American troops on R&R (rest and recuperation) from Saigon to the Philippines, Hong Kong, Bangkok, Malaysia, Hawaii, and Australia. Things had definitely slowed on the military accounts since the Paris Peace Accords, but the uptick of regularly scheduled flights in and out of Tan Son Nhut pointed to the fact that plenty of other businesses were thriving in Saigon. Al's own staff was big, and included plenty of secretaries, but he stepped out from behind a tight row of offices with beige doors to greet me himself. With a wave, he indicated that I should wind my way past the service desks to where he stood. "Glad you could make it." He clasped my outstretched hand in his and guided me toward an open office. "Take the call in here, and take all the time you need."

Thanking him, I sat down behind a desktop littered with someone else's paperwork and picked up the phone. "John Riordan here."

"It's Tom Crouse and Peter Howell here." They were important enough figures at headquarters that, although I had never met either of them in person, I knew them both by name and by title—vice president. They dispensed with any niceties and came right to the point.

"John, we want you to know that we've decided to close the bank."

"The bank?" I inquired dumbly. I knew they didn't mean New York, or any other branch. I heard what they said but was having a hard time immediately processing it. They meant to close us down in Saigon.

I drew a breath to protest but was cut off rather unceremoniously.

"We have chartered a Pan Am 747, which will arrive tomorrow at two p.m."

"That's two your time," Howell or Crouse clarified. I could no longer catch who was speaking, as I could barely make sense of what they were saying.

"Now hang on just a minute here . . . " I tried to say, but I was edged out.

"We feel that it would be appropriate for you, before you go, to take the keys and vault combination and go see the governor at the National Bank."

"If it is safe," one of them qualified.

"Oh, yes," said the other one, "only if you feel it is safe for you."

I pictured the vice presidents in their suits nodding at each other over a desk in New York.

"You need to tell him, if not verbally, at least in writing, that FNCB is officially closing its Saigon branch tomorrow."

With that, Crouse and Howell began to lecture me on the logistics: what I should do with the local staff, how I should pay them, details about the closing. I heard them say something else about my personal safety several times.

Crouse and Howell arranged the Pan Am flight, and then they gave me just twenty-four hours' notice to wind down millions of dollars of operations. They probably hadn't wanted to call me directly at the bank office because word would get out. They were afraid of panicking the local staff.

"There is no way I can do this!" I finally managed to interject. "I am not prepared to close the bank tomorrow."

I loosened my grip on the phone as they continued talking right past me. It was pointless to argue; they weren't listening to me. "We want you to take all the local staff with you, and their immediate families."

"What?" I asked, but what I meant was, "How?"

"All of you can get on the plane and fly together."

I wanted to yell at them, to raise my voice and throw a fit. How could these men tell me what to do from their offices on Park Avenue in New York City when they were so clearly oblivious to the circumstances I was in? But I swallowed my frustration at them and laid out the unpleasant facts. "Well, it's impossible. I can't take the local staff."

It wasn't that I didn't want to. If we were leaving, it would be totally wrong to leave them behind. Not only were they my friends, but they were also especially vulnerable as targets for Communist retribution. Still, it was logistically impossible to get the Vietnamese staff of FNCB Saigon on a plane the next day. "They can't get through the military checkpoints at the airport, and even if they could, they'd never make it through immigration," I explained.

I did have some clue, from the lines that morning at Pan Am and the news that managed to slip past the censors in the local English-language paper the *Saigon Post*, that people's attempts to leave the country were not going well. What I did not know was that the horrific scenes from the last flight out of Danang were all over the news in the United States and playing around the world—everywhere except here in Saigon. The already shaky South Vietnamese government was trying to stop an exodus and a surrender by default. They had put a hold on exit visas and instructed the military police to set up an unusual number of roadblocks. The state couldn't stop the rumors, though. The whispers about the numbers of people escaping by boat was lending more and more credence to the unbelievable claim that South Vietnam was at the end.

But I still didn't believe it. In my opinion, Crouse and Howell were overreacting. "This is far too early; we're safe here. It's quiet and calm in Saigon." I tried to assure them that this situation would run its course. It was just another one of those episodes that those of us in Vietnam had come to know all too well.

My certitude was met with silence. So I tried talking to them in their own language—bankers' terminology: "We're continuing to do business, and we've instituted our safety programs. The assets of the bank are secure." I ticked off the procedures we had in place to guarantee the safety of the bank's assets.

The day before, on April 2, our branch had had abnormally high withdrawal activity. One hundred and twenty million piasters in cash withdrawal was five times higher than our usual daily rate. Bank of America and Chase also had had heavy withdrawals, and the withdrawal rate at the South Vietnamese National Bank was so high that they had had to close early. The international press had picked up the story. They had tried to turn it into a story about foreign banks closing and attempted to take pictures of bank withdrawal activity at FNCB's branch. We had put a stop to the pictures, but the newsmen would have left anyway. There was nothing dramatic happening at our branch. As my telex to Hong Kong had read, "We remain in control. . . . We [are] liquid and can meet all withdrawals."

I had indicated I was ready to call some loans. I realized it would be largely symbolic—no company in Saigon was liquid enough to pay it directly—but calling loans would send a message that we would defend our assets. New York wasn't convinced. Just because things were under control now didn't mean that they would stay under control.

"John." The voice on the line was stern and damned serious sounding. "You have absolutely no choice in this matter. This is a direct order, and it comes from the highest levels of FNCB."

Nothing else needed to be said. With that, I suddenly knew the directive to close the bank had come from Walter Wriston, chief executive and chairman of FNCB. I, along with the rest of the staff, respected the man and his absolute authority. I gave in. What was I going to do anyway? I was assistant manager of one of the bank's smallest branches, and a vice president was giving me a direct order from the CEO and chairman. I had no authority on this call.

"Look," I told Howell and Crouse, "right now I am supposed to be at a meeting with the US embassy and Chase and Bank of America. I'm supposed to be telling the embassy about our concerns of the situation here."

"Well, go to the meeting," they responded. "Invite Chase and Bank of America to join you on our plane tomorrow. If they don't join you, that's up to them, but the plane is paid for by FNCB. You are taking off anyway."

The least they could do for me, I pleaded, was to delay the plane. Two p.m. was too early—I needed a few more hours so I could finish the work of shuttering the bank.

"We can give you until six p.m.," Howell and Crouse finally conceded, but advised me: "Even if you can't take anyone with you from the branch or any of the other foreign bankers . . . get on it, even if you are the only person that gets on that plane. You get on it and get out of there."

Before letting me get off the line, the vice presidents repeated themselves one more time, as if doing so would let me know that the whole New York Head Office, from the chairman on down, was of one mind about this. "John, you are closing that branch tomorrow."

"Alright," I said, and gave them my word.

CHAPTER 3

The Ides of March, 1975

U NTIL THE END OF APRIL, everything indicated that I was on an upward trajectory at the bank. I could see myself staying at FNCB for a long and successful career. In 1975, I was thirty-three years old and making a good salary as assistant manager of the Saigon branch. There had been talk of a promotion—to manager—and setting up an entirely new branch in Phnom Penh. But in January 1975, the Khmer Rouge launched a full offensive to capture the Cambodian capital. Any plans for an FNCB branch in Phnom Penh, or anywhere in Cambodia for that matter, had been shelved. Another opportunity in Asia would come along, I was told, and I had every reason to think it might.

I had been working for the First National City Bank of New York for five years. A friend from Chicago had suggested FNCB when I got out of the army and started applying for jobs in 1970. I had never heard of it since it didn't have a big Midwest presence, but I found myself in front of the bank's Head Office when I was in New York City to interview with another company. Since that interview turned out to be a flop, I thought, as long as I was in town, I might as well call on FNCB. I showed up at 399 Park Avenue at nine a.m. with my résumé in hand. The man who greeted me from the personnel department said, "You are in the right spot." He was right. I walked out of FNCB that day at five p.m. with a job offer: management trainee in the Asia Pacific Division of the International Banking Group.

The fact that I had never heard of FNCB shows what a novice I was in the banking world. It was a huge corporation with branches all over the world. If FNCB wasn't yet the largest bank in the United States, it was fast proving to be the most influential player in the financial sector. It had been the first bank to sign up with a credit card operation, and the chairman of the company, Walter Wriston, was widely considered to be a visionary. He revolutionized consumer banking, had been one of the first to see the potential in emerging market debt, and was an early adopter of using new technologies in banking. Wriston made FNCB, and then Citibank, into an emblem of American financial power.

The bank had been doing business in Asia since the turn of the twentieth century, but the whole region had been slow to recover from the ravages of World War II. Wriston wanted to expand the bank's earnings in the Far East. He regretted a mistake he had made in 1965. The bank had passed on the opportunity to open military banking facilities in South Vietnam during the war, and, as a result, Bank of America and Chase had gotten a head start in South Vietnam. My military duty in Vietnam was part of why they hired me on the spot. During my job interview they said, "We need people like you, John—people with experience over there." It certainly wasn't because of my transcript. I had flunked finance in business school; I had to repeat it to graduate. At the bank, I proved myself by learning quickly and training on the job. After a few months assisting the lead banker on the Japan desk in New York, I was sent to Osaka, Japan, followed by Manila in the Philippines.

In the fall of 1973, I got asked by Rick Wheeler, a senior vice president in New York, to think about moving to Saigon to take an assistant branch manager position. I was surprised by the offer. I had not planned on coming back to Vietnam. My fifteen months of army duty seemed more than enough time in the country. But when I thought about it, I had hated the war, not Vietnam the country. I had fond memories of living in Saigon. Coming back to it four years later, as a professional banker this time instead of as a serviceman, I found that the pace of life in South Vietnam was perfectly suited to me.

First light was my favorite time of day. All ages were up and about with the sun, brightly colored vegetables and fruit dotted makeshift market stalls, noodle sellers were pushing their carts, and the cry of the bread seller announced fresh bread for sale. As the day progressed, and the heat ripened, things slowed. South Vietnamese soldiers rolled up their sleeves and opened their shirts, dragging on their cigarettes from their posts at sandbagged observation posts. Flocks of schoolgirls on bikes floated past me on my way to work, their hair and white *ao dais* trailing behind them.

I never did mind the heat. Instead I grew fond of how people took their time doing things. After lunch most of the city was shuttered for an hour or two of *sieste*. The Vietnamese staff at the bank locked up for ninety minutes, darkened the shades, and rolled out thin straw mats to nap on the third floor. It gave me and other foreign executives time to linger with clients over lunch or take a midday swim at the Cercle Sportif, a members-only sports club. I would be back at the club most evenings if I didn't have a client event. I played some tennis but had stopped taking lessons when my instructor nudged me to quit. I wasn't getting better, and it would put him out of his misery if I would just play for fun.

My favorite bar when I was in the service was the Strawberry 4 on Tu Do Street, but it had closed in 1969 when a grenade was thrown through the door one evening. Plenty of others sprung up to replace it. Saigon had the best singers. They held long plaintive notes whether the songs were in French, Vietnamese, or English. The French had called Saigon the Pearl of the Orient, and now that I was there as a bank officer instead of a soldier, I could enjoy it. I went to fancy Chinese dinners and elegant French restaurants. I also took my clients for expensive drinks in the hotel bars with panoramic views of the city.

Alcohol fueled business relationships in Asia. I drank some Scotch or whiskey but avoided the local rice wine whenever I could. The ice chunks we were served had been chopped off of big blocks of ice, which were plunked directly on the floor of a bar or directly on the sidewalk. A slosh of warm Ba Muoi Ba 33 beer or Bière Larue cleaned the ice well enough. The beer melted off the outer layer of dirty ice, resulting in a gritty swill that was tossed on the ground or poured in an empty glass. My fingers expertly strained back the now clean ice. The bottles of beer were so large that we didn't worry about wasting a few ounces for the sake of clean ice, and the beer strong enough—foreigners called it "Saigon formaldehyde"—that diluting it was fine for the sake of a cold beer. After a couple bottles, nothing mattered much anymore—especially when the local beauties, and cuties, were so quick with a smile or with a favor.

The FNCB Saigon branch was small and still relatively new when I arrived. There were a total of thirty-seven of us on staff, including three Americans. The branch itself had opened in 1972. Some were still more certain than others about just how lucrative it could possibly be, given the last devastating decade of destruction in the country, not to mention the ongoing conflict with North Vietnam. But with the Paris Peace Accords, the war was supposed to be strictly between the Vietnamese now. The Americans were out.

The accords had been signed in January 1973, and I was optimistic enough, and ignorant enough, to believe they would hold. From a banking perspective, South Vietnam seemed like a growth market. The bank's main business in Saigon was trade finance, along with loans for working capital, equipment purchasing, and financing fixed assets. Our clients included huge international firms with a presence in South Vietnam like Caltex, Nestlé, and Foremost Dairy.

My job, as assistant manager of the branch, would be to try to help FNCB get new clients and manage our ongoing relationships. The best part of my job was the social aspect. I really enjoyed the bank's staff and our clients, and there was every indication that I was doing well, but that career was over the moment I stepped foot on a plane back to Saigon.

I had been at the beach when I first heard the news that provinces in Central Vietnam had fallen. It was supposed to have been a fun weekend jaunt to the seaside town, just a couple hours' drive from Saigon. The rainy season would start in a few weeks, and those weekend getaways were just one of what I considered to be the many perks of living in Vietnam. I had grown up in the Midwest and loved swimming in the cold fresh water of Lake Michigan. But the warm lapping waves of the South China Sea, so close to the city, with the seaside inns so cheap and plentiful, drew me to the seaside town of Vung Tau anytime I could get away.

It was a Saturday night in the middle of March, almost St. Patrick's Day. Being an Irish boy from Chicago, I can remember thinking it felt a bit like a holiday. I had been sitting in one of the open-air restaurants along the shore, drinking beer and picking apart a platter of fresh seafood with Henning Jensen, my friend visiting from

Denmark when, suddenly, the television blazed to life and caught our attention. A Vietnamese news anchor reported solemnly that the Communists had launched direct attacks on the northernmost provinces of South Vietnam as well as in the mountain areas. Improbably enough, the Communists were winning.

An image flashed onscreen of a map: Ban Me Thuot, Pleiku, Quang Tri province. These were not just some foreign names on a map. To me they were snapshots from my memory of looking out the open door of a low-flying C-130 airplane or the back of an army jeep. My memory of the Central Highlands was a thick canopy of jungle broken by impossibly green rice paddies, brown rivers, and the haze of wood smoke clinging to grey rock faces. I had been to each of these places during my time in the army. My memories seemed distant, but the immediate shock was that these were places in which my staff and friends in Saigon had grown up or had family. Now they were in Communist hands. I had no appetite to finish my dinner, and suddenly it didn't feel right to be sitting on a beach. I would have left to go back to the city that night, but I would have broken one of the first rules an American learned: it was never safe to drive on Vietnamese country roads after dark. We left first thing in the morning.

That was the beginning of the collapse, but no one knew it yet. The city carried on as normal. Restaurants were filled; ice clinked in cocktail glasses; clients showed up at the bank as usual, making deposits and applying for loans for projects that gave every indication of moving forward. The Vietnamese, and the foreigners who had been in Vietnam long enough, had grown used to uncertainty. It was our version of normal. Saigon still felt very far away from the kind of place where if you made a false step, you could be blown to bits.

The war was much more immediate for one of our staff members. Hoa returned to work from the weekend with eyes swollen from crying. She had lost her younger brother during the battle for Ban Me Thuot. He was a twenty-one-year-old soldier who had been drafted into the South Vietnamese Army after his second year studying business at University of Dalat. Hoa's brother's unit had been surrounded by the Communist army. They could have surrendered. They might have been taken prisoner, or tortured, but they might have lived. As it was, Hoa's brother refused to surrender; he fought to the end. Hoa's loss was all the more bitter because her brother had laid down his life for a war that would be over soon anyway.

Plenty of us inside Vietnam seemed convinced that this latest turmoil was just another blip in the interminable conflict. Economic, political, military woes ebbed and flowed. It only became personal when someone we knew actually lost someone to the conflict. But in the abstract, it was hard to make sense of.

On March 26, 1975, I composed a four-page telex to FNCB Hong Kong and sent a copy to FNCB Head Office in New York City. It was the first of what would become a daily message from me to the bank's management, the most basic communication of what we were seeing in Saigon. I mentioned the loss of Hoa's brother and the caution we as a staff were employing—making sure everyone was "taking all prudent measures to protect the bank." But my conclusion was that "despite all the gloom we are in complete control of bank's situation."[1]

At dinner parties and over bottles of chilled French wine, expats living in Saigon predicted a slow fall, one that, like the rest of the war, would drag on. Surely the Americans would send in reinforcements, people mused. Now that the Paris Peace Accords had been so egregiously flouted by the North Vietnamese, a new round of diplomatic talks would surely begin far from the battlefields. It was all conjecture, but it was comforting.

The part of my job in Saigon that I had liked the least was dealing with my boss, Mike McTighe. He was demanding. He wanted perfectly formatted reports in impossibly quick turnaround times. I had the impression he took some pleasure in asking for more than could be delivered. He nitpicked every report I handed in, belaboring the minutiae of the World Corporation Group's requirements for our clients. He was also the definition of a micromanager. He would check up on me during coffee breaks, and if I was missing, he'd later ask me for details of where I had been, whom I had been with, and what I had been doing. Since it was almost always something client-related, McTighe would back off, awkwardly complimenting my rapport with customers. I couldn't decipher whether the comment he included in my annual performance review was a compliment or a criticism; according to McTighe, I was still developing skills and methods "at a pace which approximates [my] apparent capacity."

I wasn't the only one who thought he was tough to work for. Others on the staff called McTighe "intense" and said he was always "looking for maximum effort, 120 percent." Although it was someone else who had called him "the boss from hell," there were plenty of days when I was sure the entire staff would have agreed.

Even so, it was clear that the branch's Vietnamese staff really admired McTighe. If he was a tough boss, he was also fair. It was no secret that FNCB paid their Vietnamese employees better than the local staff of most of the other top-tier foreign companies operating in Saigon. We all had the sense that the higher pay was because of McTighe. He was fiercely loyal to his employees.

But McTighe had been away from Saigon since late February 1975. He had taken a vacation—a ski trip to Switzerland—followed by a stop at the Head Office in New York. McTighe had appointed me to act as branch manager in his absence, and, to be honest, I had really been enjoying it. His office was much bigger than mine, complete with a private washroom and a sitting area with leather armchairs. The cream-colored smooth plaster walls and tone-on-tone striped carpeting conveyed the power and prestige of the banking institution. I got comfortable fast.

McTighe's office became the site of daily meetings with the managers of the other American banks in Saigon: Cornelius Termjin from Chase Manhattan Bank and Herman Cockerill from Bank of America. Presumably, we were just having coffee, but there was no casual bantering between us, no pleasantries or gossip from the international banking community. These were strategy meetings.

Chase and Bank of America had a much bigger presence in Vietnam than FNCB did. I wasn't so sure that our bank would have been brought in on the meetings at all if my boss, Mike McTighe, had still been there. I didn't get the impression that Cornelius and Herman liked him very much. What they did like was that our branch was small, therefore discreet.

Cornelius and Herman were always anxious that one of the Vietnamese who worked for them was going to find out that we were meeting. I couldn't quite understand their paranoia; there was nothing secret about the fact that South Vietnam was in trouble. But Cornelius and Herman blamed it on the fact that the branches of their banks were so much bigger than mine. For every Vietnamese employee we had at FNCB Saigon, they had three; we were a staff of thirty-seven, and they were over one hundred. I wasn't worried about my staff finding out. The fact was I trusted our staff. I wondered more about the clients. What would they have imagined if they saw the three of us in daily contact? Would they wonder if we were conspiring to fix prices or set rates? Or would they think that the current situation in South Vietnam had us scared?

The real reason for our coffee hour would begin from the moment Cornelius and Herman arrived in the office.

I closed the door tightly before going to the painting that hung on the south wall, across the room from the manager's desk. It was a bland scene, some European pastoral done in oil. Since I had only recently moved into his office, I had no idea if Mike had chosen it or if it had been chosen for him by the bank. But it was practical. I used both hands to take the wooden frame off the hook. The back of the painting, between the frame and the wire hanger, was the perfect place to stash a map of South Vietnam folded into quarters.

I unfolded the map onto the glass-topped brass coffee table, smoothing out the creases to lay it flat. Each province on the map was candy-colored orange, pink, yellow, or green, packed tightly into the country shaped like the bottom curve of an S. In mid-March, I had asked Chuyen to bring us a list of provinces and cities that the Communists now held. He had a family member in the military, and we marked our map with Xs accordingly. I drew them by hand but used the straight edge of a ruler to make the lines precise and defined, a futile attempt to impose order on something far beyond my control. There were always so many rumors, and when gossip combined with the news censors in Saigon, it was hard to know where the truth lay. (The map is reproduced on the front endsheet of this book.)

By the time a version of Chuyen's list made it into the *Saigon Post* at the end of the month, our coffee-hour graphics on the map marked a country collapsing in the north and to the west, moving quickly toward us.

Hue, the former imperial capital and cultural bastion of the country, was X'd out, a serious blow to South Vietnamese morale.

Danang, the country's second-largest city and home to several key military bases, was circled and X'd. The city had lasted longer than the rest of the surrounding Quang Nam province before eventually falling on Easter Sunday. X after X moved down the country, stopping at a line Cornelius had drawn with a mechanical pencil about two-thirds of the way down, linking the South China Sea to Tay Ninh on the western boundary. The new front line was less than a hundred kilometers from Saigon.

There was a shared sense among us of secrecy about the map. We hid it carefully behind the painting after every meeting so that the staff wouldn't be alarmed. Besides that, there was a real sense that the interpretation of data for ourselves, instead of relying on the American embassy or the English-language newspaper, was not approved behavior. Looking at the swift approach of our Xs toward Saigon was like looking at a time-lapse film of fate barreling toward us.

It was easier to talk frankly about what was, and what wasn't, happening in Saigon with each other than with our clients. We certainly couldn't have these kinds of conversations over unencrypted wires with headquarters back home. We were isolated and so far away. Even in good times, that played a big part in the insularity of our thinking. Bankers in Asia were awake when their superiors in the United States were asleep. We simply couldn't phone for approval of our every move. As a result, I always found managers in Asia to be more entrepreneurial and the Head Office slightly confused about what we were up to. Wriston, FNCB's chairman, referred to any arcane transaction as a "Chinese accounting system."[2] Herman and Cornelius may have had more seniority than I, but they had been equally caught off guard by the speed of developments in the Central Highlands over the last month. We were probably in the same boat as any other foreign bankers cut off from headquarters except by telex and telephone, operating on our own in Vietnam.

We had no idea what to expect next, but we thought it might be productive to band together. Cornelius, Herman, and I could wield more influence as a team than separately: when three representatives of the biggest American banks requested a briefing by the State Department in Saigon, it was in the best interest of the American government to comply.

I had been on my way to that very briefing when the call came. It was time to close the bank and get out of Saigon.

CHAPTER 4

April 3, Disaster Preparedness

A T THE END OF MARCH, Bill Walker, one of the three Americans at the Saigon branch, had thought to arrange air freight out of Saigon for his personal belongings. Walker had noticed that the Saigon classifieds, once offering piano lessons and language study, were suddenly full of cars for sale and rental villas. Companies advertised their packing services in the margins of newspapers, with cute cartoon characters asking boldly, "Going Away?" Walker got the hint and suggested McTighe and I follow him and get out one trunk of stuff, the maximum that could be shipped by air at that time. Since McTighe wasn't back from vacation, I offered to pack what I could for him at his villa.

"Don't worry too much about it, John. I just want you to take the framed picture of my dad—it's on the bureau," McTighe told me. "That's the only thing I need." I reluctantly got the framed black-and-white photo off McTighe's dresser and packed it for him in plenty of paper. Years later, his daughter, Heather McTighe, expressed surprise that the photo was the one thing McTighe wanted to take. She had always known the relations between her father and grandfather to be tension-filled; for a while they had even stopped speaking. Heather remembered hearing as a child about the items McTighe had left behind, the things he told me not to bother to take.

He lost all the photographs from his childhood and his varsity letter jacket from the Princeton crew team.

I dutifully packed up a trunk of my things, but never imagined that it would be the only thing I would have of my two years at the bank in Vietnam. Around that time, I had made up a list of everything I owned at my villa. The itemized inventory of my household goods included a marble elephant statue, Japanese paintings, a carved wooden chess set, closets full of clothing, and even a French racing bicycle in storage. True to my banker identity, I assigned a dollar value to each and was not surprised to find that the single most valuable thing I owned was my collection of books. I had about two hundred hardcover business books. I estimated that they must have been worth about $1,500. I came to regret leaving behind so much, but I am grateful for my foresight in coming up with such a detailed list. It never was clear to me whether those personal items were covered under the bank's risk insurance policy, but the bank did cover my losses. In the summer of 1975 when I returned to New York, they handed me a check for $23,887, no questions asked.

———————

Shortly after he arranged for our trunks to be shipped, Bill Walker got his family out of Saigon. Claudio, his stepson, was crying when he was picked up from school one day. The boy had been dropped off for kindergarten at the American school in Saigon as usual that morning. Walker's wife left to do the market shopping and daily errands around town. She hadn't noticed that the school was closed. Overnight, the administrators and teachers had decided to leave town and shutter the school. Too many of their students had already left town, or maybe the Communists were just too close for their comfort. In any event, the school had closed one night and did not reopen the next day. They had not told Walker's family, or presumably the families of any of the other students. For more than six hours Claudio clutched his knapsack and waited, crouched at the stoop next to the entrance of the school building, for his mother to pick him up.

As soon as Walker's superiors at the bank got wind of the story, they realized just how vulnerable their employees with families were in Saigon. That was not only an unacceptable personal risk, but a potential public relations disaster for the bank. The very next day, Walker got a telex from FNCB's regional center in Hong Kong. He had been promoted; he was needed in Hong Kong immediately.

Walker read between the lines. FNCB wasn't really promoting him, but they were giving him a way out. They couldn't directly say it had gotten too dangerous in Saigon for a man with a wife and a kid. The South Vietnamese authorities were monitoring communications, and telexes were intercepted all the time. The bank had to disguise why Walker and his family had to leave. It was the wrong moment for the bank to ruffle any more feathers, either in the South Vietnamese government or in our own.

The bank had waited about a week after the Walkers' departure to tell me that it was time to close the bank. Since I was unattached, there was no rush to get me out of Saigon, and I was fine with that. I still felt that South Vietnam had life in it. The country had come through plenty of Communist scares before. Even if South Vietnam really was on its way to the end, and to my mind, that was still a big if, it would be a slow and prolonged process. I knew my history. It had taken the Germans months of assault to try to capture Stalingrad, and the Russians held out—they had the snow to help their defenses. The South Vietnamese had a tropical monsoon season that was set to begin any moment. The Communists knew that. It would be illogical for them to begin any offensive against Saigon until after the storm season. I was sure it would take months, if not a full year. In that time, anything could happen.

The commanders of the North Vietnamese Army disagreed. A golden opportunity had materialized for them, and they were not about to let it slip away.

North and South Vietnam had been locked in conflict for decades. Before 1954, differences between the Communists and the rest of the population had been somewhat obscured, first by the turmoil of World War II, and then by a grueling nine-year war for independence from French colonial rule. From North to South, the Communists were part of a nationalist fight for an independent Vietnam. When their army, the Viet Minh, defeated the French at Dien Bien Phu in May 1954, the prospect of a Communist country scared many Vietnamese into fleeing for the South. Prosperous land-owning families knew their property would be confiscated and nationalized—or worse: collectivized. Catholics feared persecution for their religious beliefs. The Vietnamese intelligentsia had long sat on the highest rung on the social ladder. They weren't the richest, but in the traditional order of things, they were the most elite, and they feared that the topsy-turvy Communist priorities would have the proletariat ordering educated scholars to toil in rice fields.

The United States was just as fearful of the Communists in North Vietnam. It was the height of the Cold War, and the Hot War of Korea was fresh in everyone's memory. Losing another country to Communism in Asia would mean the further shrinking of the Free World, and the spread of the Soviet Red Empire.

The Geneva Accords in 1954 split Vietnam into two separate countries along the seventeenth parallel. The North would be led by

Ho Chi Minh and the Communists, while the South was supposed to be free. In a few years, there were to be elections throughout the country so that the Vietnamese people could determine their fates. But too much was at stake. The Americans poured money, resources, and men into South Vietnam to keep it from being a "falling domino." From 1965 to 1975, America spent $111 billion just on military operations in Vietnam; adjusted for inflation, that would be nearly $700 billion today.[1] That figure doesn't include the other billions in aid money for development, or the cost of outfitting a first-rate South Vietnamese Army. It also doesn't begin to cover the human cost. Nearly 4 million members of the US armed forces were deployed to Southeast Asia; of those 58,220 never came home because they were either killed or missing in action.[2] The Vietnamese cost was much higher. Although there are no official records, best estimates put the number of South Vietnamese soldier deaths at 250,000, North Vietnamese combatant casualties at 1.5 million, and civilian casualties in both countries at 4 million.[3]

Everyone was looking for an honorable way out of the war. Peace talks in Paris had started in 1968, but they moved glacially. It took eight months of negotiation just for the United States and Hanoi to agree on the shape of the conference table. When a resolution was finally reached on January 27, 1973, there was a cease-fire. The United States would withdraw its troops, and the North promised to stop sending troops into the South. But American president Richard Nixon promised the South Vietnamese that if the North did not abide by the peace, the United States would reenter the war.

It was a promise he didn't intend to keep. In August 1972, Nixon was already pessimistic about South Vietnam. "Let's be perfectly coldblooded about it," he said in a private, but recorded, conversation to Henry Kissinger. "South Vietnam is probably never going to survive anyway." Kissinger agreed but saw the situation from a practical political eye. "We've got to find some formula that holds the thing together for a year or two." Kissinger's formula became known as the Decent Interval—a period of time after the withdrawal of military troops long enough so that, in Kissinger's words, "no one will give a damn" if and when South Vietnam finally fell.[4]

The Watergate scandal helped. The United States was so bogged down in domestic political strife that there was no support whatsoever for American military reengagement to intervene in Vietnam. It was an excellent opportunity for Hanoi to act; the North realized it might not get this kind of chance again. Hundreds of thousands of troops were sent south. Some of the more cautious politburo members of the North Vietnamese government worried that such rash and obvious action would bring back the Americans, but their concerns were dismissed by Le Duan, Ho Chi Minh's successor to the Communist leadership. He felt there was no need for the North to honor the Paris agreement any longer. To his way of thinking, the South had already violated it time and time again, so the North Vietnamese incursion was perfectly legitimate. Even Le Duan was stunned at how fast, and easily, the South caved to Communist pressure in early 1975. One defeat led to another. Panic built. The country the Americans had helped build and reinforce was finally abandoned. South Vietnam would fold.[5]

But that was not yet apparent to me. After all, I had been to Vietnam before. I had arrived in Saigon as a first lieutenant, US Army Medical Service Corps (Administration), just after the Tet offensive of 1968. I saw airplane bombing, strafing, and napalming. At night I heard firefights right in Saigon. On moonless nights, the pink bursts of tracer fire would light up the sky bright as day. The closest

I came to getting killed was when I was resupplying a secret military base near Danang with medical equipment. An army lieutenant friend asked me to stay; it was already getting late, and he said the girlie dancers were coming to entertain the base that night. I said no thanks, and I went back to Saigon. It turned out that I got out just in time. Sometime in the middle of the night, the base was overrun.

When I was called back to the base the next day, I was with my boss, a doctor. We saw the devastation, though by the time I got there, the dead bodies had been removed. There were burned-out buildings and scorch marks from bombed-out areas. The doctor and I were assigned to talk to the colonel in charge of the base. We found him at the top of the water tower, firing at ghosts into the jungle surrounding Monkey Mountain. He had had a psychological breakdown. It took us hours to get him down and medivaced back to Saigon.

Because of those experiences, I thought I knew what bad looked like. To my eyes, Saigon in the spring of 1975 didn't look bad—not by any means. The city had not been overtly attacked by the Communists in seven years, and there had not even been an explosion since 1971. There was a midnight curfew, but it was not really enforced. Drunks were just shooed home by policemen. It was still a two-hour drive to anything that could be called a battle zone. In the faces of the 3.5 million people of Saigon I had yet to see any obvious panic. The only sounds of war were the three a.m. detonations set off in the Saigon River, designed to keep North Vietnamese frogmen from mining any boats.

It was easier to read the signs if you lived abroad. The American news reported daily how the South Vietnamese government and the military were falling apart. Those reports were censored in country. But even when my family sent me worried letters, I simply could not get my head around the thought that after all this time, effort, and men lost, the US government might not support the South Vietnamese when they most needed it.

————————

I had gone back to the office after the call at Pan Am, unprepared to tell the staff about closing down the branch. How would they react? How would I react if I were in their shoes? I wouldn't blame my staff if they got mad at me, I reasoned. Anger was something I could handle. I just wasn't as sure how I planned to cope with quiet devastation or disappointment. As I mulled it over, I expertly dodged shoeshine boys waving their dirty rags at me and stepped around the women in conical hats squatting near street corners—the black-market money changers. They were making a killing. I could hear them calling after me, "Lots of piasters for one dollah, mistah," but I kept moving, letting their singsong voices get swallowed by the buzz of street sounds.

FNCB had corporate policies in place for emergency bank closings. Ongoing internal discussions had been taking place within the bank since late autumn 1974, about the time the first signs of Saigon's deteriorating security situation appeared. There were contingency plans. The branch itself was a rental property, so it would simply be shuttered and locked. The central bank would take care of converting the liquid assets, and the Vietnamese staff was to be laid off. They would all be given a generous severance payment.

These policies reflected the fact that the bank had been operating in Asia since 1902. There was an institutional memory of doing business in a conflict zone. During World War II, the Japanese had interned thirty-one FNCB staff members in the Philippines. They were kept as enemy civilians in Santo Tomas camp, along with over four thousand other poor souls. The living conditions in the camp were abysmal, recalled Walter Wriston, FNCB's chairman. He hadn't been with the bank then, but was a young second lieutenant in the army who happened to be in Manila during the war. Wriston remembered going into Santo Tomas shortly after the camp had been liberated. "It was a horrible place," he shuddered as he recalled it. Wriston was adamant about keeping FNCB's employees safe from that kind of detainment under his chairmanship. He thought that if the Saigon staff members were no longer official employees of the bank, they might be safer.

FNCB had managed to maneuver its way around plenty of other political turmoil. They had survived the fall of the Qing dynasty and the Russian Revolution. It wasn't until the Chinese Revolution in 1949 that a branch of FNCB had been caught in the crossfire. The Shanghai branch had tried to continue to function during the Communist takeover of China, but the foreign exchange market had totally dried up. After one year, the bank sought permission to close. Negotiations with the local authorities broke down, and the People's Army took a hostage—Fred Harnden, Shanghai's branch manager and a British officer. The Communists demanded that FNCB pay a "liquidation tax" for his release, but of course the bank didn't want to pay it until they were sure Harnden was actually safe. Months of uncertainty followed. Harnden was released unharmed, and the "tax" was paid, but the experience left its mark on the bank, and on Walter Wriston.

"[Harnden] was the only hostage we ever had," Wriston said proudly. Since then the bank had managed to avert any situation in which staff might be at risk. In Cuba in 1959, Castro's revolutionary government had expropriated eleven of FNCB's branches throughout the country. The American bank's assets in Cuba were in the millions. The money came from sugar and land, and it had all been absorbed into

Cuba's new national bank and the Ministry of Trade. The bank lost every cent, but Wriston's point of pride was that no one on the bank's staff was hurt.[6] "When we lost Cuba, I had everybody out of there."[7]

Wriston did not want to make any mistakes in Saigon. As a matter of preparedness, our branch had already started something we called the Duplicate Records Program on March 20. Every transaction at our branch, no matter how mundane, was copied. The copies and a daily summary went out every day in an airmail pouch for Hong Kong, the site of FNCB's regional center.

Chuyen was the last person I expected to protest the bank's closing. He knew all about the bank's safety precautions because he had been an integral part of the monthly strategy meetings that had been taking place for the last six months. Chuyen knew the procedures for closing the bank as well as anyone.

But Chuyen was also well informed about the bleak security situation. His cousin did intelligence work in the Central Highlands, so Chuyen had it on good authority that the bumpy spine of the country was essentially lost—only "ghost soldiers" of the South Vietnamese Army were defending it. (They were drawing a paycheck for their families while ignoring the inevitable.) It was the first time I had seen Chuyen scared.

"You can go, but we cannot," Chuyen said in a voice that was full of regret and reproach.

"I know. Listen, I am going to see what I can do. As soon as I get to Hong Kong and get it sorted out, we will have a plan," I said apologetically. The orders to close the bank had come from the top. I couldn't ignore them.

I had deep respect for Chuyen's accomplishments, and I hated that something as superficial as a passport was standing in the way of his safety. At fifteen years old, Chuyen had left his family in North Vietnam to come south as a refugee. He wanted to make a life away from the Communists. He served in the South Vietnamese military for nine years, from 1956 to 1965, and earned college scholarships, first to San Jose State University in California and then to Tufts University in Massachusetts. As a student, Chuyen didn't intend to be a banker. He was fascinated with international studies, so he got a master's degree in law and diplomacy. But when he returned to South Vietnam in 1971, he had learned, in some ways, too much from his books. Chuyen could no longer bear the stink of his own country's corrupt politics. Without taking bribes, a civil servant's salary wasn't enough to support a family anyway.

FNCB had courted Chuyen for a position with the bank even before the branch was officially open. But Chuyen held out against the first offer. He asked for more money than the bank was prepared to offer, so he was turned down. Chuyen was pleased when FNCB came back to him with another offer six months later. They had finally matched his salary demand. It was only after Chuyen entered the banking world that he realized the bank hadn't come up that much in real terms—inflation had just surged.

Chuyen learned quickly on the job. He moved up from bank clerk to assistant manager. Chuyen's ambition was to rise even higher before his banking career was over.

When I told him about the call from New York, and that it was time to close the bank, Chuyen's black eyes flashed with angry sparks. "It's too early!"

"Well, I agree with you. But New York's ordered it, and we can't do anything about that."

"If they close the bank, we will be out of a job. The men will now be at risk for conscription into the military. It is not safe." Chuyen shook his head in disappointment. "The police and the military will trouble us."

Chuyen was not going to back down easily. He knew that he was right. If the bank closed and the employees were given severance pay, the men would most assuredly be drafted into the starved military, which was facing a looming disaster. Shutting down would also send a signal to the government. Government officials would further lose face, taking the consequences out on those who stayed behind.

So he took his argument to FNCB corporate. There were calls to New York and telexes between Hong Kong and Saigon. It didn't seem to take long before Chuyen's arguments won the right people over.

Because of him, the bank stayed open for business, and a slightly revised plan was put into action. I was still leaving, but FNCB would not totally cease all banking operations in Saigon. Chuyen would take over from me as manager. The foreign exchange side of things would close down, but since that was the most substantial piece of our business, the Saigon branch would be just a shell. All the same, it was an incredibly important one. The shell provided cover for all thirty-four South Vietnamese employees.

The bank's willingness to bend to Chuyen's reasoning showed me something remarkable was happening. FNCB was putting the safety of its people above anything else. It was an extraordinary shift. Until that point, all the communication about emergency procedures for the Saigon branch had focused solely on business and money. Now the bank was indicating that it was willing to put assets at risk if it could protect human capital. The company's generosity would continue to impress me from that moment on.

I was too busy to read the newspaper the day they called to tell me to close the bank. It was only years later that I finally took notice of the front-page article that day. When I finally read it, I laughed. That day's front page of the *Saigon Post* read: "US FIRMS IN SAIGON KEEP GOING." According to the paper, foreign companies in Saigon were maintaining a wait-and-see attitude. Someone in the press department of my own bank had commented cagily, "We wouldn't say business there [in Vietnam] is normal, but as of today, the branch is open." Indeed, thanks to Chuyen, it was.

CHAPTER 5

April 3, Money on Fire

B LACK SMOKE CURLED its way up the narrow airshaft before bil-
lowing out into the open sky. "Do you think they can smell us
on the main floor?" I asked Chuyen as I lifted another handful of
safety paper from one of the stacks. Piles of travelers' checks littered
the floor like so many ant hills.

His reply to me was lost in another whoosh of flames. The chem-
ical compounds used to treat the safety paper were especially incen-
diary and exploded into a blazing blue and orange flame when it hit
the burn pile.

It was part of the winding-down process. Chuyen and I were in
the process of burning through all the paper the bank had on hand
to issue letters of credit and to print checks. If the paper ended up in
the wrong hands, FNCB would be in the uncomfortable situation of
having to pay it out anyway. We were also burning bank forms, personnel records, ledgers, and blank passbooks. We were carrying out
orders, but it still felt wrong and strangely thrilling to be destroying
that much money at once. We burned over $1 million in travelers'
checks alone that day, but in our haste we forgot to mark down all
the serial numbers, so it was only a ballpark figure.

Just outside the window of the manager's office was a window
well. It was supposed to function as an air and light shaft, but that

day we repurposed it as a chimney. Travelers' checks, safety paper, forms, and manuals: all went into the flames dancing four feet above the gravel in the window well. It took us hours to burn everything we needed to. We learned quickly after an initial burst of frenzy that $1 million makes a hell of a fire. Without warning, the high temperatures exploded the plate-glass window in the office. Chuyen and I had turned away in time, crouching with our hands over our heads until the flames lowered. We slowed our pace after that.

Chuyen was the one who thought to stash something for a contingency plan. For the record, I hadn't actually seen it, because he had asked me to look away. But I knew exactly what he was doing. By turning away, I gave him my blessing.

Chuyen had taken two stacks of travelers' checks worth $50,000 each out of the burn pile. In the event the Communists took over the city, Chuyen realized he might not see me, or anyone else from the bank, ever again. I kept my mouth shut at the time, but when I questioned him about it years later, Chuyen had a rationale for that precise amount. Mike McTighe, the branch manager, had once told Chuyen that it was $100,000 to charter a plane for a fishing trip with clients. If the bank could write off a plane for a private fishing trip that easily, Chuyen figured, it was the least they could do to evacuate their staff in an emergency.

I had been using that office for the last month, but I still thought of it as McTighe's. Shards of glass crunched under my feet, grinding into the looped fiber of the carpet. The creamy trim around the window was scorched with smoke stains. The bank rented all three stories of the building from a local landlord. We were such good tenants that the building's owner had sent each officer our own case of Remy Martin cognac as a gift for Tet (Vietnamese New Year), but McTighe had made us give it back. It was double-dealing or somehow unethical, he said. McTighe could be a killjoy like that.

I wondered what he would make of our mess now—but only abstractly because, frankly, it was the least of my worries. I was more concerned that people on the first floor, FNCB's Saigon clients, might smell what we were up to. The acrid mix of burned chemicals, paper, and ink made my eyes burn. Chuyen's eyes behind his wire-rimmed glasses were red, but we continued to feed the flames with the bank's papers. There was nothing I could do to disguise such a blatant signal that we were getting ready to flee. How much longer did we have until the Saigon police, or the South Vietnamese Army, stopped us?

As it turned out, neither of them did. It was the American government that tried to get to us first.

I grew up on the far north side of Chicago, the second of three children. My older brother, Bill, and I were only thirteen months apart—Irish twins who were really Irish: our granddad was born in County Kerry. Our father was a Chicago police officer. He once put Bill and me in a cell, to scare us away from getting into trouble, but he never did have to worry too much about me.

I was so good in elementary school that I was chosen by the nuns to be a patrol boy. The sisters let me out of class at St. Margaret Mary's early, gave me a white sash and belt to wear, and assigned me to a street corner. I would help the smaller children cross the street, and I'd try to stop any fights. Only Sister Austin, head of the patrol boys, had a clue that I might not be as good a little Catholic boy as I appeared. She happened to look out her classroom window one day to see me dancing with another patrol boy, Bobby Goldberg, to the song "Rock, Rock, Rock Around the Clock."

My brother Bill called me "the good one" to tease me, but he really wasn't so bad either; we were just different. Bill was always playing a game with a ball or a bat, running all over town with a crew of like-minded neighborhood boys. If they got into trouble, it was for hollering too loud or breaking something. I was quieter, with a different set of friends and different ideas of fun. I didn't try to keep up with my brother because I didn't care for sports. I didn't learn how to play football until I was a grown man. Instead, as a boy, I had a real affinity for building things, like erector sets, model trains, and soapbox racing cars. I spent afternoons building forts in the vacant lot behind my house. They were elaborate constructions made out of scrap wood my friends and I had appropriated from what other people tossed out in the alley.

I liked activities that were detail-oriented, and I suppose that was good training for becoming a banker. My colleagues seemed surprised when I admitted to reading through the fine print of banking contracts. Apparently no one but the lawyers did that. The truth was I enjoyed it. I liked seeing how things got broken down into workable steps and then put back together. I suppose this makes me sound like a bit of an introvert, but I really wasn't. The best part of my job in Saigon were the client interactions. These were fascinating business people who had worked all over the world. They worked for dairy companies, oil and gas, plywood, and shrimping companies, or they were doctors and lawyers. I took my clients to the finest Chinese or French restaurants, lingered over rounds of cognac and cigars, and only when they wanted to make the night a bit longer and go to the strip clubs or opium dens in Chinatown did I beg off. This earned me the nickname "Gentle John" from my staff at FNCB in Saigon. One of my clients called me "the Preacher."

I laughed when I heard that one. I'm an atheist (although I believe in kindness and love), and I'm gay. Announcing either of those in the banking world circa 1975 would have stirred up a lot of trouble—not just for me, but for the bank too. I was never looking for any trouble. I really liked my job, and I really liked the company I worked for. Until those last hours before the bank evacuated me from Saigon, my life had been tidy, mostly quiet. People thought of me as a low-key fellow, and I erred on the safe side. It makes me think of my grandmother saying, "You know, John, quiet streams run deep." Deep enough that even I hadn't known what I was capable of.

I was in the process of updating Hong Kong on our winding-down steps when a message broke through on the telex. The machine fell into a prolonged bout of clacking. The teletype was a big heavy thing, two times the size of a typewriter on a large stand. It was isolated in a corner, separated from the rest of the office because of the din it created. I watched the words appear in front of my eyes and blinked a few times. I had never seen the machine print in red ink before.

RIORDAN, YOU ARE WANTED BY THE AMBASSADOR AT THE U.S. EMBASSY RIGHT NOW. GET OVER HERE IMMEDIATELY.

Conversations on the telex could be had in nearly real time, and although today's email makes the telex system of the past look like a clunky dinosaur, the bank relied on telex technology for decades. At the time, it seemed like a marvel of modern communication. Telexes were cheaper than long distance telephone calls and also had full legal document status. They traveled on their own networks, with their own signaling standards and exchange. There was none of the usual crackling or interference of a typical international call.

I peered at the words on the page. How strange, I thought. This message did not appear to be coming from Hong Kong. I looked over my shoulder at the empty hallway behind me and then back to the machine. Graham Martin had been the US ambassador to South Vietnam since 1973, but I had never so much as laid eyes on him before.

"PLS REPEAT MESSAGE GARBLED," I typed back.

I supposed there must have been some mistake. The ambassador had to have had much more important things to do than to meet with me. But a moment later, the machine confirmed.

YOU HAVE BEEN CALLED BY AMBASSADOR MARTIN TO COME HIS OFFICE
NEED IS URGENT

It did seem as though I were expected. When I arrived in the bank's car, a white Mercedes, we were waved right through the wide gates of the US embassy. The compound took up half a city block at the corner of Thong Nhut and Mac Dinh Chi Streets. It was about a mile from my office, right next door to the French embassy and across the street from the British embassy. With six stories, the US Embassy Chancery building was one of the tallest buildings in all of Saigon. All the windows were overlaid with a white concrete facade, a modernist look designed as much to keep the building cool by protecting it from the heat and glare of the tropical sun as it was to deter rocket attacks or grenades.

The two marine guards didn't pat me down or check me in. They simply waved the bank's driver on, nodded their closely cropped heads at me, and then showed me to the elevator. When the doors opened, I stepped directly into Ambassador Martin's office.

The room was jammed. Dozens were standing, facing away from me and toward the tall man perched on his desk. At a quick glance, I could see everyone was in a suit. There were no military uniforms here, so I assumed everyone was either a businessman or a spook. Cornelius and Herman, my coffee mates, were there, along with a few other bankers from Bank of America and Chase, but they were the only people in the room I recognized.

Herman and Cornelius knew all about the chartered Pan Am flight out of Saigon the next day. FNCB had paid for the plane, but I had invited them to come with me. Herman had been the first to respond. He had uttered a low "Goddamn" with his exhale, as if I had hit an exceptional drive off the tee at Le Golf Club de Saigon. He had conferred with Cornelius, and it was almost in unison when they declared, "We're with you!"

Apparently they had been called to see the ambassador too. The office was uncomfortably cold. The air conditioners were blasting out cold air at full force. But the full chill set in when Ambassador Martin, who had never met me before, fixed his grey eyes on me. I had read somewhere that he was famous for staring people down. He trained that gaze on me, staring over everyone else's head, as I stepped off the elevator. It was intent enough that the others in the room finally looked over their shoulders.

"Well," he said in his North Carolina accent. He made no attempt to hide that he was mocking me. "This is the man from FNCB who has a plane flying into Tan Son Nhut airport tomorrow, and is going to close his branch and leave on that plane. Isn't that right, Mr. Riordan?"

It was a rhetorical, sarcastic question. I didn't bother to explain that we were not, in fact, closing the bank completely; he wasn't waiting for my answer.

Junior staffers called Martin the "Grey Ghost" behind his back. I had heard he was an insomniac, working late into the night at both the embassy and his residence a few blocks away. He would have to be reminded of holidays, and at the end of a workday, his personal aide would get stuck with the duty of slipping him a note that read, "No one else left in the embassy."[1]

Martin had served in diplomatic posts around the world. During his time in Paris after World War II, he had been part of the contingency planning process for the evacuation of Americans and hundreds of thousands of Europeans in case the Soviets attacked. But from every account I have read of those last weeks in Saigon, it seems as though he refused to prepare for any worst-case scenarios. The ambassador was still certain that the United States would come to South Vietnam's aid, and as a result, he opposed any suggestion of early evacuation. It would be alarmist, he said, and bad for South Vietnamese morale.[2]

The Vietnam War was personal for Ambassador Martin. In 1966, his son was killed when his helicopter was struck down by a .50-caliber round in the Central Highlands. Another son was tragically killed on the day of his college graduation in a car accident, when he lost control of the sports car Martin had given him as a graduation present. By the time I met him that day in 1975, the politician who had once identified as a New Deal liberal had hardened. His disdain of "disaffected intellectuals" was well known. He thought of journalists and professors at liberal arts colleges as "Lenin's league of useful idiots," doing the work of the Communists for them.[3]

In that way, he reminded me of a colonel from my army service in 1968. I had been in Washington, DC, at the time, serving at the office of the army's surgeon general. Colonel McBride called me to his office one morning to tell me he had solved the problem of what to do with the hippies from Haight Ashbury.

"We're going to send them to the front lines!" he boomed. "Vietnam! What do you think about that, Johnny?"

I thought he was joking, "Oh Colonel, I don't think that is a good idea," I replied lightly. "You know, I'm from Chicago, and I've always voted for the Chicago Cubs." He understood by my answer that I cheered for the underdogs—which made him pretty damn mad.

"Oh, so you don't think it's a good idea?" he had said tartly, and before I could say another word, he ordered me out of his office. "Coffee time is over. Get your butt out of my office." I scrambled out of there, and two weeks later, I found out I was reassigned to Vietnam.

I was not happy about the idea, and my parents were worried too. I went to see McBride at his house before I left. I held out my hand to the colonel, and he shook it, telling me before we parted, "Remember, Johnny, I got you the good job over there."

The year 1968 was the peak of US involvement in Vietnam. The North Vietnamese had launched the Tet Offensive, a series of attacks that caught everyone by surprise. One week in mid-February had set the record for the highest casualty toll of American soldiers for the whole war, and it looked like things were only getting worse. When my parents brought me to O'Hare Airport in Chicago to see me off, it was the only time I can remember my father kissing me. In those days, we normally just shook hands. He was also crying—another rare sight. It was only the second time I can remember seeing him cry; the other time was when our dog Captain died. When my father said good-bye to me at the airport, he must have been thinking, *I'll never see this kid again.*

As it turned out, thanks to Colonel McBride, I did have a relatively good job in Vietnam. I was assigned to SOG (Studies and Observations Group). The tame and scientific-sounding name concealed the fact that SOG was a secret, elite unit of the military. There were Army Green Berets, US Air Force Commandos, and Navy Seals, but the SOG unit didn't exist on any of the military's organizational charts. I was a noncombatant in charge of medical supplies for secret bases that carried out interdiction missions. I wore civilian clothes much of the time and lived in bachelor officer quarters near the Central Market. When I traveled to base camps throughout the country, near the borders of Laos, Cambodia, and North Vietnam, it was usually a day trip.

But I had come close enough to getting fired on a few times, and the experience changed me. Before the army, I was afraid of the consequences that might be doled out by authorities. My dad told me stories from his job as a cop, and I could all too well picture what it was like to get into trouble.

I remember driving around Mississippi in the summer of 1965. I was visiting a former girlfriend who was with a civil rights group registering African American voters. I was twenty-three years old. Civil rights was a cause I believed in fully, but when I got pulled over by a Mississippi state trooper, he growled at me: "Do yourself a favor, boy—put your foot on that gas pedal, and get your ass outta here." I had been cowed by the uniform and the holster into complying. But things changed once I had the experience of being in a uniform myself. Maybe it was because during my service in Vietnam, when death was all around me, I got a new perspective of what "scary" really was. Or maybe it was because I learned about chains of command. Now that I was out of the army, my commands came from my bosses at the bank, and so did my paycheck. When I found myself in the ambassador's office in Saigon, I was not as easily scared away by anyone claiming to be an authority.

I found the ambassador condescending and rude. He was mocking me with his sarcastic tone. I held my head high and looked right back into Martin's famous grey eyes.

He didn't look scary to me; he looked a bit ill actually. I would learn later that the ambassador was taking large doses of antibiotics to treat pneumonia and fight off bronchitis, and to me he looked like a man with the weight of the world on his shoulders. There were large circles under his eyes and crags in his face.

Seeing that he couldn't push me around with the authority bit, Martin tried on some of his Southern charm for me. "Well, look," he said with a smile. "I want you to cancel that plane, and I want you to come to my house and have dinner with Mrs. Martin and me tonight. We'll talk about all this."

"Mr. Ambassador, I'm afraid I cannot do that." All eyes were on me, disbelieving my gall in standing up to the official representative of the US government, the man handpicked by President Ford to speak for him in Saigon. And yet it felt perfectly natural to me: this man was not my boss. What could he do to me? "I've been ordered by FNCB New York to close our Saigon branch. I'm closing it. The plane is arriving here tomorrow. I am going to be on it." The words flowed out of me with confidence and conviction.

Martin's face puffed red and radiated anger. If the American banks left, it would look terrible for him. Martin's story was that everything was going to be fine. Nobody should panic. He gave me a long glare, throwing daggers with it, but the effect bounced right off me, which must have made him even angrier.

He wasn't used to being ignored. The ambassador reached out both his hands and motioned as though he were dipping them in an imaginary bowl of water. He methodically washed them and mimed toweling off, and then he spoke: "That's what I feel about you guys. I wash my hands of you. I don't give a fuck what happens to you. You will get absolutely no support from me, or the United States government." Martin drew a breath to compose himself, and the flash of malice in his eyes flickered and died. He continued in a disappointed tone: "Close your banks, if that's what you feel you've got to do. But," he concluded, "I think you are precipitating the fall of Vietnam."

There wasn't another word said. I was dismissed.

Icouldn't quite believe that I had stood up to the ambassador of the United States. *Was it a punishable offense?* I belatedly wondered. Here I was, thirty-three years old, in a Saigon that was growing increasingly surrounded by sworn enemies of the United States, and I had just been told that my country was washing its hands of me. Well, I reasoned, even though the representative of America didn't approve, at least I had the bank to protect me.

I lived about a mile away from the branch, and I remember my walk home from work that night. I was trying to keep my mind focused on the immediate task of following the bank's orders to shut down part of the branch and get out. The checklist of everything I needed to do was still long, but some thoughts were nagging me. If Martin had such a problem with Americans leaving, how would the South Vietnamese ever get out of their own country? What was the right way for America to leave the country we had fought so hard to keep free? We couldn't underwrite their struggle forever, but it didn't feel right to abandon such a vulnerable ally.

Along the way home, Saigon's streets were draped with propaganda banners, long banners of yellow fabric with red letters—the national colors of South Vietnam. They heralded President Thieu's "Four Nos," a set of precepts dating from the Paris Peace Accords, when America pulled out the troops. It was supposed to be a nationalist morale booster, "No negotiating with the enemy, No Communist activity in the South, No coalition government," and the one that had been most obviously, and recently, violated, "No square inch of the national territory is to be abandoned to Communists."[4]

I had a healthy level of cynicism when it came to government; after all, I did grow up in Chicago. But the Vietnam War was a lightning rod in American politics, and money was a huge part of the problem. The American people were fed up with their tax dollars going to fund a war they were tired of. The 1975 energy crisis meant that gas stations in the United States were closed on Sunday, and there were long lines every other day of the week. A gallon of gas had quadrupled in price. A three star general had summed it up neatly during a visit with the CIA Saigon station chief, Thomas Polgar: "I'll be goddamned if the U.S. government should be sending money to Saigon to buy gasoline so these f'ing cowboys can ride around Saigon on their Hondas while my wife has to wait in line for an hour to get a tankful of gas."[5]

In early January, after the first province in South Vietnam had fallen to the Communists, the Ford administration had asked Congress for $300 million in supplemental military aid. They had already slashed the budget for military and economic assistance in South Vietnam for 1975, approving only half of what had been asked for. Requisitions for fuel, weapons, and ammunition were kicked back. Saigon was desperate for more funds, so of course, it made sense that they would play up how badly things were going without enough assistance. But all the posturing for funds obscured the truth. Was it really that bad, or was the Saigon government just trying to get more money?

A joint team of US Senate and House members had come to Saigon at the end of February. In theory, they were coming to see for themselves the facts on the ground before reporting back to Congress. I was invited to meet them at a cocktail party, and I had to admit I was not very impressed with the men and women dispatched on the fact-finding mission. For the most part, they had already made up their minds about South Vietnam.

History writer George J. Veith would describe the congressional visit as "disastrous," "buffoonery," and a "new low in American diplomacy." From what I saw at the party that night, I had to agree. Bella Abzug, the hat-wearing firebrand from New York, complained loudly about the humidity and the heat. Someone else whined about how the accommodations in Saigon were not up to their standards. It was supposed to be an occasion for the congressional delegation to get acquainted with the situation in South Vietnam, but instead of listening, they seemed intent on making it clear to those of us living in Saigon how anxious they were to return home. There was only one, Representative Paul McCloskey from California, who seemed genuinely interested in hearing how the Paris Peace Accords were being implemented. He was a major critic of the war but came away "surprised by the success [and] capability of the [South] Vietnamese army. Vietnamization has succeeded from a military standpoint. It is a superb fighting force." Nevertheless, his conclusion was still to discontinue aid because, no matter what, McCloskey believed that "the North Vietnamese are going to win."[6]

After the visit, the summary recommendation of the group was that the US government should cut off military aid to the South Vietnamese government. The practical effects wouldn't be visible for a few months; I supposed that was because there were enough supplies in the pipeline. But the psychological effect was immediate. If morale was shattered for the South, it had to be boosted for the North.

I sympathized with Ambassador Martin: he had a tough job and a hell of a fine line to walk between the Ford administration and the antiwar legislature. But in every account I have read of those final weeks in Saigon, Ambassador Martin comes across as someone who refused time and time again to face reality. He's like the boy in the Hans Christian Andersen story who thinks he can save the town from flooding by sticking his finger in a dike.

After the meeting with Ambassador Martin, I received a telex summarizing the discussion at the embassy: "The U.S. ambassador was approached with a request to assist the three banks in evacuating their total Vietnamese staff plus immediate families." Given the absence of passports and exit permits, the banks requested that the embassy "arrange with the Vietnamese government for the necessary documents." If things really got bad enough, the banks asked if the embassy would agree to "assist the three banks in circumnavigating the laws governing the emigration of Vietnamese nationals from Vietnam."

The answer was no. Martin had denied both requests. His only concession was to offer assistance to senior Vietnamese staff members, "should that become necessary." The problem lay in determining if and when the situation was truly critical.

When I read the memo that was supposed to sum up the meeting, I couldn't quite believe what I was reading. The language was diplomatic and nonconfrontational. It read like a different meeting from the one I had actually attended. What I witnessed was Martin in a mean mood and nothing but disagreeable to any suggestion that the banks might try to help their staff get out of the country.

I would have agreed with Martin on the most important point, and that was that South Vietnam had some fight left in it. Outwardly, things were so much quieter than they had been in 1968 and 1969. I did not think all was lost. But unlike the ambassador, I didn't have all the facts in front of me. I didn't have expert reports and military studies. Instead I had an embassy that was feeding me false information, and on purpose. They were doing so to avoid demoralizing the remaining shreds of the South Vietnamese government. I was right when my gut said not to trust them.

CHAPTER 6

April 4, Leaving Saigon

I TASKED A MARKETING OFFICER, Robert Chang, with breaking the news I was leaving to the rest of the staff. The word around the bank was that Robert was some kind of local VIP. He was young and seemed to have effortlessly fused street-style cool with the traditional buttoned-up banker's suit. Robert was the oldest son of one of Saigon's richest Chinese businessmen, and somehow or other, he had avoided the draft. The fact that a young man his age was off the front lines confirmed he had the connections and the cash. I found out later that Robert also had a Taiwanese passport.

Robert carried himself like someone of importance. When he didn't feel like doing something, he didn't. I was relieved when he agreed to speak to the staff on my behalf. It wasn't just my leaving that I asked him to communicate; I also wanted Robert to find out who would want to come with me. It was not an easy thing to do.

I chose my words carefully before saying, "Robert, would you try to find out who would want to leave the country, if they could? Some might rather stay in Saigon, and take their chances. . . . " But I couldn't imagine anyone taking that option, and my voice trailing off gave it away.

Robert smirked and commented, "That's a delicate situation."

I nodded. To come right out and ask the staff if they wanted to leave would be illegal. Under current South Vietnamese rules, it would be treason. We ran the risk of offending someone loyal to the faltering government, someone who would inform on us. Although we had worked together and knew each other fairly well, everyone had heard the rumors of people who had been double-crossed by loyal friends—and not just by reporting them to the South Vietnamese government. Communist agents were everywhere. But Robert accepted it in stride. For his whole life he had been discreet. As it would turn out, every member of the staff told Robert that they wanted to be evacuated, as long as their families were too.

Lien was our senior clerk typist. Her hair fell like silk curtains around her shoulders, and her smile could light up a room. Lien was petrified of the Communist advance. She had already fled the Communists once, as a young girl growing up in North Vietnam. She was born in 1943, in the midst of the Japanese occupation of Vietnam during World War II. The Japanese requisitioned crops from the Vietnamese farmers and demanded that they grow jute instead of rice. It caused a terrible famine that killed over two million people. Lien was the seventh of nine children, but four of her siblings died. After her father died, the rest of her childhood was spent on the run in the jungle, moving around from town to town, village to village, during the war between the French and the Viet Minh. In 1954, after the Geneva Agreement was signed and the country divided in two, her family relocated to the South as refugees.

Lien quit school to work for MACV, the American Military Assistance Command in Vietnam. Her steady salary helped her mother pay for her siblings' education. At twenty-two, Lien fell in love with a fighter pilot in the South Vietnamese air force. He was overseas, in the United States for F-5 fighter pilot training, when Lien gave birth to their first son. Always careful with money, Lien got a job as a teller with one of Bank of America's military banking facilities at an airbase. She came to FNCB after the airbase was destroyed by mortar fire in early December 1972.

At the first signs that the government in South Vietnam was losing control, Lien was already panicking. Would she have to go back to living in the jungle, on the run from the Communists with her three young boys?

Robert gently asked her, "If the bank couldn't take the whole family, would you go alone?"

Lien shook her head vehemently. "I would never leave without my children."

"Would you be willing to take the children if your husband couldn't leave?"

Lien choked back her tears. "I will have to discuss it with him," she managed to say before crumbling into tears.

No one said that administrative processing was easy. I was grateful Robert was the one asking the questions that we felt had to be asked.

The bank had decided that even if it wasn't completely closing its doors, the branch was on borrowed time. One of my last tasks before leaving the bank was to approve the payout of six months of severance. The money seemed to make people more nervous. Maybe they thought the payments were the bank's way of easing its conscience, or that money absolved the bank of being further responsible for the staff. Then there was the problem of the pay itself. In two months, much less six months, the piaster currency could be nothing but worthless paper.

I wrote a letter to the Central Bank of South Vietnam, forward dated two days, to April 5, 1975. "Since it is necessary for me to visit Hong Kong for consultations, Mr. U. D. Chuyen . . . will take my place as Acting General Manager, effective today." I gave Chuyen the keys to the vault and a firm handshake along with the promise that I would do everything I could to get him and the staff out.

One more dramatic moment took place in mid-afternoon on Friday, a few hours before I left the bank. Betty had come in to tell me I had a call. When I picked it up, I heard a frantic American voice on the line.

"John, are you OK?"

"Fine, yes—who is this?" I asked calmly.

It was a banker from Chase Bank. He was part of a small group that had flown in from Hong Kong to help Cornelius wind down Chase's operations in Saigon.

"Aren't you leaving with me in a few hours for the flight back to Hong Kong?" I asked, but the voice kept asking me if everything was alright.

After the third time they asked, I exploded: "Goddamn it, of course I am OK. What is this? I am busy!"

"Don't move," said the voice on the other line. "Stay exactly where you are. We'll be right over."

I would have done anything to get off the phone with them at that point, so I said, "Fine," sharply and hung up. I had no idea what was going on.

Not five minutes later, two Americans from Chase were at the FNCB branch. They flew into my office and looked around crazily. Then they closed the door tightly behind them and asked me again, "John, are you OK?"

I scraped the chair in my haste to push back from the desk and stood up. "Do I not look OK?" I asked peevishly.

The men looked at each other and then back at me. "Look," they said, and began to explain a circus of phone calls from one bank to another, all taking place without my knowledge. "We got a report at Chase from Bank of America's office in Thailand. They said your staff had rebelled, and"—one of them cleared his throat out of either anxiety or embarrassment—"that your secretary had stabbed you."

I roared laughing at the idea of the five-foot-one and honey-voiced Betty attacking anyone with a knife. Her family had fled North Vietnam in 1954, when Betty was twelve, because they were devout Catholics afraid of religious persecution. "Do I look like I've been stabbed? Does it look like a rebellion around here?"

They agreed that it did not. "It is a strange day in Saigon," one of the men from Chase muttered. I had to agree with him on that one.

The plane had been downgraded from a Pan Am 747 to a 707 once it was confirmed that we really couldn't get our Vietnamese colleagues out. FNCB had paid $70,000 to get this plane here, and there were enough seats for 150 passengers. I was glad I had asked the staff of Chase and Bank of America to join me, but even with the others, we only filled ten seats. We had a captain, a copilot, and an engineer for the plane, and we also had three flight attendants—all for the ten of us on a two-and-a-half-hour flight to Hong Kong.

Al Topping, the Pan Am director, was waiting for me at the foot of the stairs: "Where have you been?"

It was not quite six p.m. Mr. Hanh, the bank's driver, was able to drive right out onto the tarmac at Tan Son Nhut—right up to the stairs to the plane. We had gone easily through two checkpoints, manned by the national police and the South Vietnamese military. I wasn't late, but Al was fidgeting. "I was waiting for the other bankers downtown. We were supposed to rendezvous there and come out here together," I tried to explain.

"Well, they've been on board for an hour and a half!" Topping exclaimed. I said a hasty good-bye and clambered up the stairs to find a seat. I stowed my small suitcase and a briefcase, settled into a row of seats I had to myself, and ordered a beer from the flight attendant.

I don't remember talking to Al about anything else. We shook hands and parted ways. I was exhausted and drained from the whirlwind winding down of the branch. If Al were acting strange, I barely noticed. It was only later, when I learned about the horrific accident that had taken place just three hours earlier, that I thought back to Al, and everything he must have been dealing with. And I realized, my God, it had been a miracle we got out at all.

A few hours before our plane took off from Tan Son Nhut that Friday, the first flight of Operation Babylift took off from Saigon. A $2 million special foreign aid and children's fund had been authorized by President Ford to get 70,000 children out of Vietnam. There were to be thirty flights from Saigon to destinations in the United States, Europe, and Australia. Many of the kids were *bui doi*, "dust of life," meaning they were of mixed race. These were war orphans or children who had been given up by their families in the hope that they would find a better life outside of Vietnam. It was feared that multiracial children would face a life of discrimination in Vietnam, if not outright retribution by the Communists. One Vietnamese mother said she was so afraid that her daughter would "be soaked with gasoline and be burnt" by the Communists that she felt she had no choice but to give up her child.[1] Before takeoff, all of the children had already been adopted by expectant foreign parents.

The first plane they filled with children was a large military transport aircraft, a C-5 A Galaxy, the world's biggest at the time. It was jammed. The youngest ones were belted into rows of cardboard boxes on the upper level of the plane, a pillow and milk or juice snuggled next to them.

The American ambassador, Graham Martin, must have realized that a goodwill effort on behalf of orphaned children would reflect nicely on the US government. He publicly said that the evacuation "would help reverse the current of American public opinion to the advantage of the Republic of Vietnam."[2] Privately, people said Martin had been slow to warm to the idea.

Disaster struck shortly after takeoff. The rear doors blew out, two hydraulic systems went down, and the captain was forced to crash-land the aircraft in a rice paddy just a few hundred feet from the runway. While 176 survived the wreckage, another 138 children and volunteer adults accompanying them died. It was the ones on the upper level, the younger ones, who survived at a higher rate. The lower level was almost completely destroyed in the fiery crash.

By the time I saw him at the stairs to our chartered plane on Friday evening, Al Topping already knew about the tragedy. In fact, he was scrambling to mobilize Pan Am aircraft to help. Within hours, two of Pan Am's Boeing 747s had been chartered by Holt International. They would depart Saigon with the survivors of the crash and sixty volunteer escorts. The planes also carried nine crew members and hundreds of bassinets, diapers, and bottles of formula. Each child wore a white ID band on one arm with their name and case number and, on the other, the adopting parents' names and the child's destination, like San Francisco, Chicago, or New York.

With Al's help, those thirty-hour flights would land safely on the West Coast. Including the children brought by Pan Am, a total of 2,300 Vietnamese children were brought to safety over the next two weeks, but that was just a fraction of those who wanted to get out.

The American government had not come up with the idea for Operation Babylift all on its own. An unofficial evacuation of children had started the week before, an effort spearheaded by Ed Daly, the copilot of the Danang "flight out of hell." Daly was known as a maverick. Someone described him to me once as a swashbuckling hero; another called him an impulsive drunk. He thought of himself as the "Wyatt Earp of the airline industry."[3] Say what you like about his character, he was worth millions.

When his daughter told him about the plight of so many children in Vietnam, Daly personally arranged one of his planes to evacuate the children and negotiated with the charities running the orphanages, paying for the whole thing out of his own pocket. But at the last minute, he was nearly thwarted by the American embassy and Ambassador Martin. The embassy told the charities that Daly's plane was unsafe. It was unpressurized, they said, and had no toilets, neither of which was true. Charles Patterson, Daly's vice president at World Airways, believed that the embassy spread those lies on purpose to interfere with the children's rescue because they didn't want to be shown up by a character like Ed Daly. He had made the Americans look bad enough in Danang.

According to Patterson,

Graham Martin was very concerned that nothing go out or happen that would give him further problems of convincing Americans that the damn place was about to fall. You recall during those days he was still trying to project the image that we were going to stand there and that things were going to work out. It was my impression that

70

the idea of somebody as flamboyant as [Daly], who had also been to Da Nang, flying a load of orphans into California was going to pull the stopper on any effort that they might have to convince the American people and the government in Washington that this was still a viable situation. So I think that had a lot to do with it.

Ed Daly managed to fly out sixty orphans, and his actions did convince the US government that someone had to step in to do the right thing for the children. Martin eventually came around, and Ford's $2 million special allocation was speedily approved. But Patterson was still unflinching in his assessment of the actions by the embassy in Saigon: "The American government did arrange to fly those orphans out, and they flew them on that C5 that crashed. So a lot of the kids we were supposed to have taken were killed."[4]

Our plane must have flown right over the wreckage, but none of us knew anything about the tragedy until we got to Hong Kong. Instead, we used the flight to unwind. I got very relaxed after a few beers. I am pretty sure we all did, since there were only peanuts and booze available on that flight. Alcohol released us from the last, tense thirty-six hours.

We landed, taxied in, and were told that a herd of press people were waiting for us. The ten of us represented the fact that the three biggest American banks had left Saigon—that was a story. But it was not a story any reporters were going to get that night. Once the FNCB people from Hong Kong saw the shape we were in after a few drinks, the press conference was cancelled.

We were shuttled instead to FNCB tower in downtown Hong Kong, where lots of coffee was brewing. I stayed up half the night, filling in the details of what was—or more accurately, what was not—happening in Saigon. I helped prepare a nearly coherent press release, one that was vague enough that it wouldn't endanger our staff but precise enough to explain why I had left. Word had spread quickly that the three American banks had removed their foreign staff and greatly reduced their Vietnam operations. There was surprise—and some animosity—from other American businesses with operations in Saigon. They felt the banks had pulled out too quickly, and the fact that we didn't discuss it with the American Chamber of Commerce first really rankled. It was hard to believe it had only been a few days since Ambassador Martin had scolded me in his office, telling me that by leaving South Vietnam, the bank was precipitating the fall of the country. As Martin had predicted, in the days after we left, the remaining foreign companies in Saigon began to collapse their operations and evacuate their non-Vietnamese staff. The already fragile South Vietnamese morale was shattering.

I also finally caught up on the news from Vietnam. It was news that we in Saigon had not been allowed to see, presumably for our own good.

That was when all the letters I had received in the last week made more sense. The Easter card from my always optimistic mother had been particularly perplexing:

John Dear,
It's difficult to say happy cheery Easter words when you are living under such troubled conditions—our prayers are for the well-being and safety of your friends and for all those trapped in this frightful

senseless war—there are no words I can offer that would have
much meaning. We love you and pray for you.

I had sent nothing home to indicate that the bank was closing. How could I? I had only just found out myself, and I still didn't think things were that bad.

My friend Shunzoh in Japan had sent a few lines, including nothing about my birthday, which I had thought was a strange oversight for him:

Dear John,
Are you all right? Are you out of danger? . . . I am worried about
you. . . . I saw thousands of refugees fleeing from Hue today. Please
let me know that you are alright.

I didn't know what news was making it to the United States. The news in Hong Kong was uncensored, so I learned much more about Vietnam from there than I ever had on the ground, but we also got all sorts of misinformation. There were rumors of North Vietnamese death squads and rumors that secret negotiations were under way to divide the country. People said all the South Vietnamese military posts were abandoned because the soldiers just wanted to rescue their families. Someone told me about a report on the radio that China was invading, and all the North Vietnamese troops were being recalled to fight a new war on the border. I was sure that some of the stories I was hearing were actually planted as a last-ditch measure to try to trick the enemy. Black propaganda was something my SOG unit had used in the military, and the radio was incredibly effective at reinforcing what the enemy already believed. In the case of the North Vietnamese, their long-standing suspicion of the Chinese might have been enough to send troops back to the North, and away from Saigon, to protect their land from an invasion from the north. Common sense told me not to believe anything I heard.

From Chepy, a Filipino friend in Washington, DC, I did get a birthday card, and also a note written in a tense script:

> *If we are to believe what the newspapers say then the situation there must be bad. . . . It looks like it is getting out of hand. . . . I wonder what the people think [will] happen? What is your parents' reaction?*

I had replied earnestly to everyone that I was fine, that everything was fine. I brushed off their concerns. My everyday life was not the one at risk. What was uncertain was the fate of the FNCB staff still in Saigon.

CHAPTER 7

April 5–12, Hong Kong

F ROM THE MOMENT I landed in Hong Kong, I was back at work. My first task was to help reconstruct the books of the Saigon branch, but since we had been sending microfilm copies of every transaction, that wasn't too hard. I also spent some time on actual bank business. Chuyen was running things in Saigon, but he forwarded some of the work to Hong Kong. There were hard questions from Vietnamese clients who wondered about the security of their deposits, and also from the staff. They called in with questions about how to run through the daily transactions of the bank with frozen assets, a nonconvertible currency, and not enough liquidity to pay out those clients who wanted to close their accounts and get out. The question that was on everyone's mind but remained unasked was, *How are you going to get us out?*

Years later, I asked my Vietnamese colleagues what they remembered about working at the bank in Saigon while I was in Hong Kong.

Thi Dau said, "Everywhere people tried to find [a] way to get out of the country. People tried to hide gold in the seams of their pants or anywhere they felt it safe. At the bank, people looked worried."

Xuan in the credit department recalled the day our tellers were told to recommend to small-account holders to close their accounts.

She had already heard about my burning the bank passbooks before I left, so when Xuan was told to microfilm all the customer loan account files to be sent out of Saigon, she thought the end was at hand. "At the end of the workday when I witnessed all the abnormal actions, I could not walk to the bus station." Xuan recalled that she had been physically paralyzed by fear: "I called a taxi and was crying all the way home as I thought that the Communists were coming soon to South Vietnam."

Oanh, a customer service representative, watched an unusual amount of commotion with Chuyen, Robert, and Huy running back and forth, up and down the stairs, many times a day. "I saw it all without knowing what was going on." She finally asked Robert, and he told her the bank was drawing up plans for an evacuation, but not to tell other people about it. By "other people" she couldn't be sure if he meant in general or other bankers. "Nobody trusted anybody."

Thi Coi remembered that the bank was especially crowded, with people lined up to withdraw money for their escape plans. "In town, everywhere, people discussed the cost of purchasing a means to run away, either by ship, by boat, by anything."

I moved into room 1444 of the Hong Kong Hilton. It was conveniently located across the street from the FNCB tower, which had been completed just a year before. The new tower was supposed to represent the best of modern architecture, but its black shiny windows and cylindrical shape reminded me of nothing so much as an upright roll of thirty-five-millimeter film. FNCB's Hong Kong staff had cleared some desks for us, and we set up a temporary space dedicated to the Saigon branch.

While rummaging through old files for this book, I found a stack of notes I can vaguely remember having written while sitting at one of those desks in the FNCB tower. There are dozens of pages of notes in my handwriting on the back of lined ledger paper. Some of the pages are in a neat tight script, others in a big scrawl. I had drawn a map of the area surrounding the airport, noting where the police checkpoints were, and a rough sketch of the bank's proximity to the US embassy and the presidential palace. Looking through the notes brings a knot to my stomach even now—the anxiety of those tense weeks, trying any plan, no matter how crazy, expensive, or desperate, anything to try to get the Saigon staff out of South Vietnam.

In Hong Kong I found myself reunited with my boss, Mike McTighe. We got along better there than we ever had in Saigon. We had found ourselves a common focus. McTighe was no longer the one giving me impossible tasks to complete or questioning my reports just to make himself heard. We were in the same boat, fighting for the same thing, the safety of the Saigon staff. McTighe put aside his usual lone wolf act and collaborated on every phone call and every plan. We were so joined that I couldn't help but find myself questioning if he were still my boss.

The man was as odd as ever. He had a habit of going into trances and at the most inopportune times. He would go staring off into space, or worse, zone in on someone's face without really seeing them. It was as if he drew a curtain and went away for a while. In Saigon, when one of McTighe's blank episodes would take over, I would kick him, or shove his elbow, hoping that no client had noticed and that Mike would come back to earth. Who knew what he was thinking during these episodes. But in his absence from the office, I had gotten out of the habit of watching for them.

"All my life, I've been a maverick," he once said to me, and it was true that sociability was not one of McTighe's strong suits. The former marine deplored anything but the straightest talk. When he thought of something, McTighe usually came right out and said it before thinking about the consequences. At first glance, that kind of impulsiveness seemed to contradict his pedigreed education. McTighe was a product of two of the finest East Coast schools, Exeter and Princeton, where he rowed varsity crew and joined the Ivy Club. His father was a lawyer, and his mother, Esther, was a writer for *Vanity Fair* magazine. He was their only child, but it was not an easy childhood. McTighe's parents were alcoholics. If he were close to anyone in his family, it was on his mother's side, a bunch of Norwegian cousins who lived all the way across the country in San Diego. McTighe was a lonely, if not prideful, kid from New York City. He developed a chip on his shoulder from all that time trying to fit in with the East Coast Brahmin blue bloods during an awkward adolescence.

By the time I knew him, McTighe had earned a reputation at the bank for being tough on his contemporaries and vicious with his put-downs. He had self-sabotaged more than one opportunity to rise up the corporate ladder. In a bank that measured success by how well employees worked together on a team and helped each other out, McTighe was open about the fact that he marched to his own drummer. For as bright as he was, and as hardworking as he was, McTighe remained unpredictable and an outsider.

I had wondered why McTighe never came back from vacation, but McTighe was tight-lipped about it. Upper management had told him to "stay put" was all he would say.

I thought the bank's directive that McTighe not return to Saigon was a measure of corporate concern for an employee's safety, but I found out later that it was because of McTighe's famously disruptive nature. FNCB's management was scared of sending McTighe back to Saigon. It would have been like sending in a grenade with a loose pin. He could scare the bank's clients, or he might piss off the South Vietnamese government. No one could say with any certainty what McTighe might do, and that made him dangerous. I didn't know it then, but McTighe had inherited his parents' addiction. He was struggling with his own alcoholism. We all drank a lot in Saigon; that just seemed to be how business got done in Asia. The pressure to drink didn't come from the Americans living abroad as much as it came from our Asian clients. I saw McTighe hungover a few times. He had a quiet, pained look and slouched shoulders, but I never thought much of it. It was par for the course in the banking industry in Asia. I felt pretty bad a few mornings myself. In any case, I cannot ever remember seeing McTighe out-of-control drunk.

Whether he was drinking or not, the bankers at FNCB Hong Kong thought McTighe had been acting twitchy. It seemed as if he might decide to take it upon himself to head back to Saigon just as the rest of the bank management was coming to a consensus that it was time to get me out and wind down the branch. Dick Frey-tag, FNCB vice president and senior officer for the region, had dis-patched a group of his deputies to the Hong Kong Hilton to try to talk McTighe down, but things had not gone well. I heard it from one of the deputies who had been there. He was an older gentleman who worked under Freytag, and he spoke with an Irish brogue. He told me the story over drinks one night like a sports announcer call-ing a game. He may have embellished some of the details, but the picture he painted for me was comic:

McTighe started to run away. His tie was loose, his shirt was un-tucked, and he was holding his passport like an Olympic torch, run-ning down the hallway of the hotel. Two of the deputies started to give chase; they had to tackle him to get him to stop running. They wrestled McTighe's passport out of his hands, and that was the end. The bank was holding on to the passport. McTighe had no way out until they said so.

Hong Kong should have been a great place to be based. We were living high above the bustle of the city in five-star accommodations at the Hilton, among tourists and other businessmen, ensconced in modern rooms with every amenity. The hotel had a terraced garden and a swimming pool with a view of junks and sampans sailing through the harbor. My room was on the other side of the hotel. It looked straight into the heart of Central in Hong Kong, the city's teeming business district.

The dark glass tower of FNCB was just a shard among other skyscrapers, part of a concrete city for a modern economy that had been carved onto rocky promontories. I was told it was just like Monte Carlo, but that reference held nothing for me, since I had never been there. I was also told that the old days of *The World of Suzie Wong* were gone, but with a short ferry ride across the harbor I was lost in the charms of the old-fashioned Chinese city on Temple Street.[1] The crush of humanity was in Mong Kok, alive with the smells of joss sticks and exha   fumes. At night the neon signs for dim sum and cocktail lounges were brighter than the light of day. It was all fascinating and wonderful, and I could see why it was such a popular port of call. I was there on R&R in 1968, spending time eating and touring and shopping. But with all my worry for the bank staff stuck in Saigon, I was not permitting myself a moment to enjoy it.

On Sunday morning I saw Dick Freytag heading out of the bank, out of his usual suit and dressed for a day of sailing.

"How can you go off sailing at a time like this?" I asked him in an accusatory tone.

He just looked back at me with real empathy. I had been sleeping on the floor of his office, waiting for some call. My hair was mussed, and I couldn't remember the last time I had sat down to a proper meal. I was too tense to eat and too worried that I might miss a call. I was working day and night, all the time, on any scheme that might help our Saigon staff.

Freytag said, "John, it's Sunday. Everyone needs a day off." Of course, he was right. For all the tension and pent-up anxiety over the fate of the staff in Saigon, in Hong Kong there was absolutely nothing to do but wait for the phone to ring. Someone, however, had to do the waiting, and I was glad to take it on. As Freytag left for his outing on the harbor that morning, he said to me reassuringly, "You've got the conn, John." I nodded but had no idea what he meant until someone who had been in the navy explained it to me. The "conn" means the conduct, or control, of the various parts of a ship. Freytag was using the term to let me know that I was on important duty, standing conning officer watch.

The first plan that I helped come up with to evacuate the bank's Vietnamese staff involved chartering another commercial plane, this one from Trans International Airways. The plane would fly from Seattle to Tokyo to refuel before coming to pick me up in Hong Kong. I would fly into Saigon with a briefcase full of money, $70,000 in US dollars, freshly withdrawn from the Hong Kong vault. The money was to bribe whoever might be bribable. I had notes on where to get fake passports and papers, $6,500 per person.

The charter had filed a flight plan from Seattle. It was standard procedure and might have slipped through the cracks, but someone caught wind of it. The authorities in Saigon let the plane get as far as Tokyo before they sent the flight crew a message: their plane would be confiscated by the South Vietnamese government if it tried to land at Tan Son Nhut. The pilot had no choice but to turn the plane around and go back to Seattle.

Plan B quickly came together. FNCB's petroleum department in New York knew that a Sun Oil exploration ship was operating in the Sulu Sea, just off the coast of the Philippines. The ship had a helicopter landing pad. Since Sun Oil and FNCB had a substantial relationship, the oil company agreed to let us have the oil-drilling ship equipped with a helicopter landing pad. All we needed were the helicopters. After hours on the telephone and telex, in coordination with FNCB's airline department and the aerospace department in New York, and with the support of senior officers in FNCB Tokyo, we secured three Sikorsky helicopters based in Bangkok from All Nippon Airways. They could hold sixty people each.

We still needed to find a place for the choppers to land in the city. Rooftop evacuation posed logistical issues, but Saigon had plenty of open parks. In dire need, even a city park would work, so we decided to go for it. The real complication with any helicopter plan was that the ship had room for only one chopper at a time, and we had plans for three coming in, one right after the other. The only solution seemed to be an expensive one, to dispose of the helicopters after we had used them. One chopper would land, let the people off, and then get dumped off the helipad into the sea to make room for the next helicopter. FNCB was willing to spend as much money as needed.

The details had solidified enough so that the Sun Oil ship actually started moving out of the Sulu Sea. It began repositioning closer to the Vietnam coast to be within fuel range for the helicopters when the Philippine navy got in its way. The Marcos government refused to get involved in the turmoil of Vietnam. It was unmoved that Sun Oil was a private corporation—President Marcos was sure the South Vietnamese government would see it the same. The Philippine government ordered its navy to block the Sun Oil ship. If Sun Oil ever wanted to do business in Philippine waters again, there was no choice but to comply. The ship went back to the Sulu Sea.

Back in Saigon, Chuyen had been in almost daily contact with Jim Ashida, the economic attaché in the American embassy. They had talked through various procedures for evacuating the staff, but the lack of exit visas remained an insurmountable hurdle. Ashida told Chuyen not to worry: when the time came, the embassy would take care of American companies' employees in Saigon. But he was also clear that his hands were tied as long as the ambassador, Graham Martin, remained stubbornly against any evacuation plan. Off the record, Ashida communicated to Chuyen that we should not pin all our hopes on the embassy. "You should have your own private alternatives."

The embassy may have had good intentions, but it was very clear that it was not going to risk upsetting the South Vietnamese government by advocating the departure of its citizens, no matter who their bosses were. For all the embassy's talk of emergency protocol and evacuation routes, it was baloney.

"We cannot depend on the United States embassy," Chuyen concluded. "They will create chaos. If they do anything, it will be very last minute." McTighe and I wholly agreed, but with one plan falling apart after the other and us stuck in Hong Kong, it was looking as if we might not be able to do anything about it.

I was about a week into my Hong Kong stay when McTighe made use of his Marine Corps contacts. They got us in touch with an American named Jim Eckes. On paper, Eckes was just another airline guy running cargo planes in and around Southeast Asia. But Eckes had distinguished his company, Continental Air, as being the charter airline of the CIA. His planes ran agents around Vietnam, Cambodia, and Laos. It was only years later that I found out that Eckes was so fearless because he didn't just contract out to the CIA; he himself was an agency man. The official CIA line was that the agency was not involved in any illegal movement of people, but one thing about Eckes was clear: he could get in and out of the country with no questions asked.[2]

Our first meeting had had a clandestine feel. Eckes had knocked on my Hong Kong hotel room door at three in the morning. McTighe was already waiting with me, and he motioned Eckes to come in. I had wheeled the desk chair around for our visitor to sit, but he shook his head, so we all remained standing.

Mike had been the one to walk him through the story so far. "Thirty-four employees of our bank and their families are still in Saigon," McTighe explained. "There's over a hundred of them in all. They've got no immigration papers, and no exit visas."

Eckes nodded along. It wasn't the first time he had heard this kind of story. "Alright. I can help you." The man spoke without a discernible accent and quietly, as if he didn't want to be overheard. The creases in his face suggested that he had a few years on me, but it may have been a few years of living hard. His eyes were set too closely together to be considered handsome, but they were his only distinguishing feature. Otherwise the man was nondescript. He wore light-colored slacks and a pressed shirt with thin stripes. To my eye, there was nothing about him that was outwardly remarkable, but McTighe found him captivating. I could tell by the way McTighe leaned in for Eckes's every word. For once, he was completely focused. His eyes were bright and wide, like a little boy's on Christmas Eve. McTighe loved this kind of cloak-and-dagger stuff.

"My fee is $50,000." The money was to be wired to a Swiss bank account, but only if, and when, Eckes got our people safely out of Saigon.

Eckes and McTighe came up with the concept of a "feasibility study" to appease FNCB's Head Office. We expected them to be skittish about putting trust in someone like Eckes. He was a self-proclaimed aviation expert—in other words, a wild card. The bank's chairman, Walter Wriston, and his top staff had not given up on the idea of going through official channels. They had friends in Washington, and they would try calling together all the banks and American companies with branches in Saigon to get Secretary of State Kissinger and President Ford to declare a national emergency. In that case, the American embassy would have to act. But whatever enthusiasm the bank officials managed to generate in Washington was stymied by Martin's stubborn nature. The ambassador insisted that it was far too early to call anything an emergency. He would not let them give up on Saigon.

FNCB's main concern, officially stated, was always the safety of the staff. This was reiterated by every one of the senior managers at the bank, from the senior regional officer Dick Freytag on down. In one of the meetings, I remember hearing, "We don't want any discussions, with anyone, about strategies that we cannot guarantee, 100 percent certain."

But as the days in April were slipping by, it became clear, at least to McTighe and me, that there was no such thing as complete certainty. The most Eckes would concede was, "I won't undertake any plan unless I am 95 percent certain."

To McTighe and me, that seemed perfectly logical. Eckes's price did seem reasonable, and there was the bonus of the gentlemen's contract—paying only for success. McTighe and I didn't see any harm in having a man like Eckes on our side. So we agreed to Eckes's terms with a handshake in the middle of the night. There was no reason to tell anyone else at the bank about our deal, McTighe convinced me. Eckes would be our secret weapon, to be deployed only in a worst-case scenario.

I thought the meeting was concluded. I made my way toward the door to let Eckes out of my hotel room so I could get some sleep. But before I could open it, Eckes put his hand out, signaling he wasn't quite finished. "I've got only one condition," he said. "If you do this through me, I'm going to need a contact on the ground in Saigon—someone I've already met, and someone I can trust." Eckes looked pointedly at McTighe and then at me. That was the first time I thought about going back to Vietnam.

CHAPTER 8

April 14, Saigon Briefings

JIM ECKES WASN'T THE only one who wanted an American FNCB contact back in Saigon. At the end of the second week of April, the US embassy in Saigon formally invited the bank to send one staff member to South Vietnam. The chosen representative would receive a day of top-level briefings. From the embassy's perspective, it was a chance to prevail on the American commercial interests in Saigon to keep a cool head. For the bank, it was a due diligence trip, a chance to kick the tires on whatever emergency plans the embassy might have in place for the staff.

It was also seen as something of an olive branch. My first and only meeting with Ambassador Martin before leaving the country had been a disaster, albeit not one of my making. It was in the interest of both the bank and the embassy to smooth things over.

In Hong Kong, a few of us were called into the office of the regional senior officer for a meeting with Dick Freytag. He explained, "We've been able to prevail on the US government to be more cooperative . . . and we have been invited by the United States embassy in Saigon to send one representative of FNCB back to Saigon. He won't need to do anything, just go in there and listen to what they have to say." Also at the meeting were Mike McTighe and Bill Walker, FNCB Saigon's head of operations, who had preceded me to Hong Kong by a few days. Freytag, in consultation with George Vojta, the executive vice president and head of FNCB's international banking division in New York, thought it might help FNCB's Vietnamese staff if we could get back on Martin's good side, but they admitted that they were still torn, given the fact that the bank had spent $70,000 to fly me out of Saigon just ten days earlier.

I looked around the room and considered the options. Walker was married with a young son, and McTighe was without a passport, so he was grounded. None of the other bankers in Hong Kong had any experience in Saigon.

I was it. I had the experience, and I was unattached. FNCB had a tradition of recruiting bachelors for employment in the bank's international operations. It used to be that managers looked with "disfavor" on any employee who married without the consent of his district vice president, at least until he had been in the bank's service for five years. Those regulations were actually written down somewhere, but this was 1975. All that was left of that rule was an unspoken sense that a young man should not take on family responsibilities until he had proven himself.[1]

Though the bank's policies had been moderated and reformed, there were still at least two important constraints for employees. These were unwritten, but biases all the same. One discouraged marriage between an American banker employed overseas and a local woman. That didn't apply to me, but the other policy did. Later in my banking career I knew people who had sat in on promotion meetings. Supposedly, if a male candidate for promotion to vice president or higher was unmarried, it wasn't uncommon for the others in the room to question his sexual orientation. Being gay was an impediment to promotion. I wasn't open about my sexuality back then, but no one really asked. I had to look for other ways to impress the senior management.

Those kinds of strategic career decisions were far from my mind in Freytag's Hong Kong office. There was simply no time. Freytag and the other bank officers were looking at me expectantly. Would I go back to Saigon? A quick gut check was all it took.

"Okay," I said matter-of-factly. "I'll do it."

After I volunteered, it struck me that I was carrying out something of a family tradition.

My mother's brothers, the Murphy boys, had been missionary priests in China. It had seemed exotic to me as a young boy. They would come home to my grandmother's dining table in Chicago with stories of their adventures. They had sailed over on a boat from Vancouver to Peking and wove tales of their life there as if they were from the pages of an adventure book. They dashed around the teeming city in rickshaws or on motorcycles, bicycles, and even donkeys. Their mission sites were schools and orphanages, but they also told stories about the bandit hideouts in the mountains. Their mission had intensified with the Japanese invasion of China and the beginning of the Sino-Japanese War in 1937.

We called one of our uncles, Clarence, by his nickname, Slug—a diminutive of Slugger. Clarence had been a crack baseball player before going off to seminary. Family lore has it that he was even scouted by the Chicago White Sox but chose the priesthood anyway.

Slug was the priest in a Chinese parish church on the outskirts of Peking during World War II. If any American flyers who came into his region were downed, the Chinese would bring the airmen to Slug. They knew he would take care of them. One time he was hiding a bunch of US military men in the church, when the Japanese started sniffing around. Slug and the military men got out just in time by scaling over the back wall.

Slug managed to get away a few times from the Japanese but not from the Communists. In 1949, he was taken prisoner by the

Red Army. Slug stayed in a Communist concentration camp for one horrible year. When he was finally released and sent back to Chicago, he made it his life's purpose to try to get back to China, but his bishop said no—Slug's order, the Vincentians, would not send him back in.

As his family, we understood his call to the mission. Slug felt he had to do all he could to fight against the Communists in China, and for him, that was ministering to the millions of Chinese who would have to bend to Communist rule. But anyone not related to us must have thought Slug had gone slightly bonkers from his time in captivity. Who in their right mind would choose to go back into a country in such turmoil?

I had no fear of going back to Saigon. I felt that my going would do some good to repair relations between the bank and the embassy.

Freytag had made sure to clarify my choice: "You know, you can say no, and that would be the end of it."

I knew that no one would think less of me if I chose not to go back to Saigon, but the truth was I felt fine about it. Maybe I felt a little responsible for whatever acrimony my departure had caused. And I still felt that people were prone to overreaction when it came to the situation in Saigon. This would be the trip that changed my mind.

The bank booked me a round-trip ticket from Hong Kong to Saigon on April 14. I was to fly in and then back out on the same day; it seemed safer that way. I had three meetings set up with different government officials, a whirlwind fact-finding mission in the space of a few hours.

The day got off to a good start. Wolf Lehmann, the embassy's deputy chief of mission, greeted me in the main building of Saigon's airport with a handshake. His smile at seeing me seemed genuine. It was such a change from the way I had been dismissed by Ambassador Martin in the American embassy before I left. "I apologize for our approach and attitude when you left Saigon and for the ambassador's way of treating you and the rest of the bankers," Lehmann said, and his tone was contrite. "It has been a pretty trying time for us."

Lehmann and I knew each other casually. His home had been the site of the cocktail party I had attended back in February, when he had hosted the disappointing group of congressional delegates. That evening had ended on a sour note for Lehmann. He and Paul McCloskey, the seemingly serious representative from California, had gotten into a terrific argument. McCloskey threatened to subpoena the diplomat, and Lehmann had raged at him to "go ahead and do it already," before storming away and ending the party.[2]

I could appreciate the difficulty of Lehmann's situation. And I was impressed that Lehmann had taken the time to apologize—he seemed to have been otherwise rushing through the airport. Whether he had been coming or going, I couldn't tell, but I found out later that Lehmann was the main reason that American planes were still flying in and out of Vietnam. Earlier that week, the Federal Aviation Agency in Washington had decided, without a word of warning, to declare the Tan Son Nhut airport no longer safe for American commercial aircraft. Lehmann had recognized that this was the kind of thing that would set off a panic the moment it became public and took it upon himself to bypass it. Lehmann called the White House and got the National Security Council to rescind the FAA declaration. This was the kind of man who could get things done.[3]

"What can you do to help us get our local staff out?" I asked Lehmann at the airport. When he assured me that the embassy would do all it could, I believed him.

It had been decided that Jim Ashida, the embassy's economic attaché, would accompany me to the various appointments. Ashida had been in daily contact with Chuyen at our branch ever since I had flown out of Saigon on April 4, so he knew the bank's situation well. The fifty-five-year-old career diplomat smiled at me and briskly suggested we get on our way, setting the tone for the officially optimistic tour I was to be given.

The first meeting of the day was in the political section of the US embassy. The open floor plan had dozens of people sitting underneath fluorescent lights at desks stacked with paper and files. All those industrious young staffers reminded me of the New York Head Office of FNCB. Two officers brought me to a desk stacked with boxes full of continuous-feed printer paper, with paper spilling out. The text on each page was single-spaced, in small, black, tightly packed type.

"This is a list of 627,000 Vietnamese names. They are all prioritized for departure," the embassy staffer explained.

"Are all of FNCB's Vietnamese employees in here?" I asked incredulously.

"Well, yes, but you can, of course, confirm."

No, really, I couldn't. It was a needle in a haystack. There were too many boxes to count, and I didn't have the time. Besides, I didn't know most of the staff's full Vietnamese names. Many of them went by Americanized versions for bank business. To my untrained eye, it was unclear to me how Anh Tuyet and Mong Chi ever became Betty and Yolande, but I was glad for the help. There was also the issue of first names and last names. In Vietnam, the family name comes first, followed by the middle name, and then the given name. But at the bank, we inverted the order to more closely match that of American names, and even then people had nicknames. I didn't know how the embassy had everyone listed—Americanized name or Vietnamese name? Vietnamese name order or American?

It seemed completely overwhelming to me, but the officers bobbed their heads, assuring me up and down that the US government was going to be able to get all of these 627,000 individuals out of South Vietnam. It was an organizational feat of wonder. There was a list and, presumably, some sort of plan, but I found little comfort in the thought. Something seemed suspicious to me, even if I couldn't very well argue it.

I was whisked off to my next briefing, this one with a CIA officer. Ashida and I were ushered into a windowless room in another wing of the embassy. We were the only ones in the room, along with the intelligence officer, but he put on quite a show. His projector flashed country maps and statistics on troop buildups around South Vietnam. It boiled down to this, he told me: The CIA had intelligence operatives throughout the country. Their information was that the South Vietnamese military was still strong. "Of course the United States is still supporting them," he confided, "and the advancing North Vietnamese troops are now at a distinct disadvantage. They moved too quickly; they've outpaced their supply operations."

It would be at least six more months before anything serious happened to Saigon, the officer guaranteed. I listened politely and made mental notes on the statistics he had presented. But all that optimism rang hollow. A queasy knot formed in my gut. Instinct told me that this was too good to be true.

For my last briefing, Ashida and I took an embassy vehicle out to Tan Son Nhut airport. The embassy's military attaché, US Army Colonel Charles Wahle, had moved his office out of the embassy compound. Reportedly, he and Ambassador Martin had not been getting along. I knew what that was like.

Colonel Wahle had installed himself at an office in the Defense Attaché's Office. The DAO was the principal US military head-quarters remaining in Saigon after Military Assistance Command, Vietnam, was disbanded in April 1973. The office's main function was arranging the delivery of US military aid, but it also had an in-telligence role, trying to keep track of developments in the military situation. The DAO's nickname was Pentagon East. I was familiar enough with it from my days in the army, but I couldn't have imag-ined how well I would get to know the place in the week to come.

The DAO's huge grey buildings were behind a high fence and adjacent to Tan Son Nhut airport. I could look out at the tarmac where my plane would be taxiing off for the flight back to Hong Kong in just a few more hours.

Ashida approached the secretary's desk outside Colonel Wahle's office and introduced me: "This is Mr. Riordan from FNCB Saigon. The ambassador sent him. He's to be briefed by Colonel Wahle about the military situation."

"I'll let the colonel know." The secretary excused herself and slipped into the colonel's office, leaving the door ajar.

We heard Colonel Wahle before we saw him. He boomed from inside his office: "I have no goddamn time to be giving bankers any briefings."

Ashida tried his diplomatic best, moving ahead of me into the office. He spoke courteously, but his words cut right to the point: "The ambassador insists you give Mr. Riordan a briefing."

I listened in on the exchange between the two embassy attachés with unabashed interest. My escort for the day could keep his cool because he had the trump card. The ambassador had ordered this briefing. Even if Colonel Wahle didn't like Martin, he knew the ambassador could pull rank.

"Ok, send him in here. I've got sixty seconds for him."

I walked in and said hello, but the colonel made no time for pleasantries.

"Don't sit down," he ordered me. "This will be quick. Here's the story: They have ten divisions surrounding the city. We have two defending the city. Do you see that plane on the tarmac out there?" Without waiting for an answer he continued, "Get your ass out of this office and onto that plane. Get the hell out of this country as fast as you can."

Ashida and I stared at the colonel, but he seemed to have forgotten us as he dropped back down into the seat at his desk to confront a pile of papers in front of him. When he finally noticed us still standing around, the colonel barked at us, "Get the hell out of here—now!"

Colonel Wahle was the first authentic voice I had heard all day. The meetings at the embassy had gone on for an hour or longer, but it had taken sixty seconds at the DAO for the colonel to make his case. I knew the truth as soon as I heard it.

Colonel Wahle would be a minor figure in books about the American evacuation of South Vietnam, but in my mind, his speech was decisive. I wouldn't find out until later that the colonel had been trying to warn anyone he could about Saigon's imminent fall. He had been involved in the evacuation of Danang and knew how quickly things could get bad. The colonel had been on the record since Easter Sunday saying, "This thing is not going to last much longer."[4] But as I had already found out firsthand, the ambassador did not like people to contradict his knowledge of South Vietnam. He kept Colonel Wahle as quiet as he could.

Ashida threw his hands up in the air. I thought he was going to scold Wahle for going against the embassy's line, but something about the colonel's finite tone had unmoored the State Department employee. Ashida was stammering, "But the ambassador says we have nothing to worry about. I have my family here, my household. My wife and children!"

Wahle nearly floored the diminutive Ashida with his roared response: "Well, get your ass in gear and get them out of here."

I left Saigon and went back to Hong Kong on the Air Vietnam flight that afternoon. I relayed the day's meetings to Freytag. He had been joined by George Vojta, the head of all of the bank's international banking operations, who had just flown in from New York. I told them that the embassy was officially optimistic. "But if you want my opinion," I ventured, "we better get our staff out of there." I believed Colonel Wahle. We were running out of time. Vojta nodded that he understood. He didn't have me write up any report; he was just glad to have me back, he said.

The other bosses in New York had gotten very upset when they found out I had gone back to Saigon. It had gone all the way to Walter Wriston, the chairman of the bank. He had given Vojta a terrible time about authorizing my return, however brief and however well intended. "My ass is grass," Vojta told me without cracking a smile.

CHAPTER 9

April 17,
Dinner in Hong Kong

T HE LONG ASH COLLECTING on McTighe's cigarette was a dead
giveaway that he had gone off into one of his trances. It was
terrible timing. We were in the senior officers' conference room of
the FNCB tower in Hong Kong to discuss the situation in Vietnam.
It was the end of the work day on Thursday, April 17. Three days had
passed since my one-day trip to Saigon before Vojta called us in for
another meeting.

We all wore lightweight suits and a serious look. McTighe sat
with us and was physically present, but he stayed a bit apart. That
aloofness was characteristic, as was the carefully combed blond hair,
his trademark. McTighe had a habit of checking his hair in the mirror before going anywhere, pulling the ever-present comb out of his
pocket to curb any misaligned strands. Seemingly nothing was out
of place, except McTighe in general still seemed uncomfortable sitting there. Maybe he already knew what was coming.

Vojta didn't bother to sit down with us. Neither did Freytag. He
just stood behind Vojta. The senior officers obviously had some important directive; they were presenting a united front. Vojta was the
one who spoke, addressing McTighe, Walker, and me carefully. He
had bad news to deliver.

"Look, we've done enough. We've done all we could. We've tried very hard." Vojta recited our failed attempts: the chartered plane, the helicopters, and the ship stopped by the Philippine navy. Vojta had encouraged all these plans, and by the way he played with the knot in his tie as he spoke, we could see it was hard for him to break the news to us that it was over. "There just aren't any alternatives."

Out of the corner of my eye, I could see McTighe without having to turn and look at him. The Vietnamese staff had a theory about McTighe's moods. They said you could tell when he was getting mad because his face would get red. I thought I knew McTighe well enough by then; I thought I knew that he would be passionate about getting the staff out. He should be mad as hell at Vojta's speech—there just had to be alternative plans to evacuate the staff. But Mc-Tighe simply sat there, pulling absent-mindedly on his cigarette.

Vojta was going on and on about how much the bank had tried to pressure Congress and the White House. So far, everything FNCB had tried was to no avail.

"The decision from the highest level of the bank is that we need to put our trust in the United States government. They have made us promises. We need to rely on our government that they are telling us that they are going to get our people out."

I couldn't hold my tongue another minute. I addressed my senior FNCB officer as directly as I could while still being respectful: "George, we don't believe those promises. We know that the ambassador is out of touch with reality. He's not even getting along with his staff."

It was too crude to call outright bullshit on the embassy in the bank's meeting room, but that's what it was. I thought of all the crazy ideas and haphazard plans that the bank was trying to orchestrate. The embassy should have had plans for something like this; that was what it was there for.

It took me a moment to compose my temper. What difference did it make? It was useless to dwell on something that was already past.

"I know how you feel, John." Vojta looked at me with sympathy. "But this is the decision. Whatever's going to be done from here on is going to be done by the United States government."

Vojta took his eyes off of me and paced a tight circle. "None of you are to go back to Saigon under any circumstances. If you do, you go back on your own. Do you understand?" If we did go back, we would not work for FNCB anymore.

He stopped in front of Freytag and said, "Dick, I want you to understand that if you try to go back to help this effort, you are going back on your own." Freytag nodded solemnly. Vojta took a few more steps until he was standing behind the table and directly in front of McTighe. "I want the answer from you, McTighe. Do you understand?"

McTighe managed to come back from whatever far-off place he had been. "Yes," he said, grinding out his cigarette butt in the ashtray.

Vojta moved to Walker, where he got another yes, before coming to a stop in front of me. "John, do you understand the order from the bank that you are not to go back to Saigon?"

"Yes," I repeated. I understood.

I must have looked pretty dejected after that meeting because McTighe came up to me and said, "You know, John, you've done such a great job here." It was a voice I wasn't used to hearing him use—encouraging and almost fatherly. I really appreciated it.

McTighe and I walked into the bank corridor together. We had shaken hands with Vojta and Freytag, and Walker had made his way past us with a quick wave. He was going to check on the operations side of things before going back to his family for the night. McTighe and I had nothing left to do. In one sense, all the pressure to rescue our staff had been lifted off of us. If we had felt relief, it would have been understandable. At the very least, McTighe and I should have been exhausted. But instead, I felt uncomfortable to be so suddenly without purpose.

McTighe must have felt the same.

"I'd like to buy you dinner tonight," McTighe offered. "Would you have dinner with me?"

Wow. Isn't that nice? I thought. *This son of a gun wants to treat me to dinner, after all we've been through.* It was thoughtful, and it was the last thing I expected. "Thanks, I'd like that."

"Where would you like to go?"

I would have been happy slurping up a bowl of noodles from a market stall down the road, but I didn't think that was what McTighe had in mind. I was so flattered he had asked me to dinner and to pick the place; I wanted to make it something we both might enjoy.

"How about that steak house over at the Hilton?" I suggested.

McTighe smiled at my choice. The Grill at six thirty it would be.

We went back to our own separate hotel rooms to clean up. Until then, McTighe and I had practically been roommates in the Hong Kong Hilton. Despite the hotel's vast size and its nine hundred rooms, we had taken to sharing one with twin beds. That way one of us would always be awake to man the phone. It was ringing at all hours with calls from New York and Tokyo and Manila. Even then, it didn't always work. McTighe would pick up the phone in the middle of the night, mumbling "Yes, sure, yes," into the receiver. When I asked him about it the next day, he didn't even remember getting out of bed to take the call. The same thing happened to me once or twice. The middle-of-the-night calls had been coming in from FNCB branches all over the world in every time zone. Everyone had been trying to help us find a way to help the Saigon staff. Every one of their plans had failed.

There was no point in us sharing a room anymore. There would be no more middle-of-the-night phone calls to Seattle arranging charter planes. We were through with procuring helicopters from Thailand or routing oil exploration ships from the Philippines. If it were really all over and done, I wondered what was going to be next for me. Would the bank post me back to New York, or somewhere else in Asia? It felt strange to think about the future—as if I were being selfish, not knowing what was happening to Chuyen and Chi and Betty and the rest of the staff back in Saigon. But what was I supposed to do about it? The bank had tied my hands. I might not like it, but I had to accept it.

———————————

The Hong Kong Hilton had at least half a dozen different restaurants and lounges on site. The Eagle's Nest was a restaurant on the twenty-fifth floor with floor-to-ceiling windows and sweeping panoramic views. It was the kind of place you would go if you had something to celebrate; Mike and I were definitely not in a celebratory mood. Below street level was the Opium Den Bar. It had been a popular watering hole with the soldiers on R&R during the war. That might have been a place where we could have drowned our sorrows, but it was too depressing. The Grill was something in between. It was quiet and refined, like a men's club; even the decor was polished wood and brass. The smell of chops and steak greeted me as soon as I opened the door and made my mouth water. I realized how much I was looking forward to a steak dinner and some Scotch.

This was the kind of evening I had enjoyed on a regular basis with my bank clients, and I suddenly realized how much I had missed it. I hated to admit it to myself, but it felt good to leave the struggles in Saigon behind and enjoy a night off.

We started with a round of drinks. The clink of ice in our glasses overshadowed any small talk. McTighe wasn't one to talk about the weather anyway, and he didn't gossip. He just sipped persistently at his drink while he looked at the menu. Meanwhile, I kept pace with my Scotch. There were deep cushions on the seats and pressed linen napkins; I was enjoying myself immensely. I paid no attention to what McTighe ordered. I zeroed in and chose a giant cut of beef that would be served with a green vegetable and potatoes.

I already had my fork in one hand and a thick-handled steak knife in the other the moment the waiter set my steak down in front of me. I was poised to pierce the crust, ready to sink my teeth into a well-deserved treat of rare and juicy meat, when McTighe got my attention with a throat-clearing *harrumph*. I grinned up at him. I thought maybe this was another toast to our efforts. Instead, McTighe dropped his voice to a quiet register and told me why I was really there.

"You know, John, one of us has to go back."

The truth of it knocked the wind out of me. I carefully set the silverware back down, fork on the left, knife on the right, and pushed the steak away. The smell that seemed so tantalizing a moment ago now flooded my nostrils, the bite of ground pepper overwhelming me completely. A wall of tears surged but held fast just behind my eyelids.

McTighe leaned in as if he had something to confide, but he just slipped into the rebel routine. "You see, I've been a maverick all my life in this bank," he began, but I shook my head. I knew where he was going with this. One fat tear escaped and slipped down the side of my nose.

McTighe kept on talking about his career at FNCB as if he hadn't noticed. "If I go back there, they're gonna fire me. No doubt about it. They really hate me. And we just can't send Walker—he's got a wife and a child. He just got them out—you helped get them out—we can't ask him to go back."

None of us could go back, not if we wanted to keep our jobs. McTighe knew it as well as I did. Not even three hours had passed since we had sat in the conference room in the FNCB tower. All of us had promised Vojta that we understood, that we would not go back into South Vietnam as FNCB employees.

McTighe took a bite of his food and chewed on a wad of meat. He was trying to avoid watching me steady myself. I could feel a wet track down my cheeks. I didn't trust my voice to say so right away, but of course he was right. One of us had to go back. We couldn't leave our staff there. There were thirty-four employees and all their families. I didn't know for sure what would happen to them if the Communists came, but I knew it wouldn't be good. And I knew what they thought was going to happen. If the Communists came to South Vietnam, the employees of our American bank believed that they, and their families, would be severely punished, if not killed. That was the worst part. The thought of them feeling so scared and abandoned. McTighe was right, and I knew it. One of us had to go back. It was the right thing to do.

But it still wasn't easy. I had a good job with FNCB. It was a wonderful old banking institution, and it was an exciting time to work for it. Wriston was redefining modern banking practically single-handedly. Plus it was one hell of a cushy job. I liked it and was doing well enough to think that I was on my way up the corporate ladder. *I'm going to give all that up* was all I could think of.

I was thinking through all these things over my cooling slab of meat. McTighe kept chewing his steak, pausing only to take a sip from his drink and swipe a napkin across his mouth. I was only a bit younger than he—seven years—but he was pushing me around as if he were an old man. His family situation was a consideration in my mind. I didn't know much about his personal life, but someone had told me he had an ex-wife and child in the United States to support. He couldn't risk his job, or his life, and besides, he still didn't have his passport back.

I finally spoke: "Okay." Once I found my voice, the tears retreated. My decision was made, and that was it: I was going back to Saigon. I walked away from that beautiful steak without taking a bite.

At the same time I was making up my mind to go back to Saigon, a cable was coming into the American embassy in Saigon. It was for Ambassador Martin from the White House. I couldn't have known about it. The memo was classified, sensitive, and exclusively eyes only.

WHITE HOUSE 50717

SENSITIVE EXCLUSIVELY EYES ONLY VIA MARTIN CHANNELS

TO: AMBASSADOR MARTIN
FROM: HENRY A. KISSINGER APRIL 17, 1975

WE HAVE JUST COMPLTED [sic] AN INTERAGENCY REVIEW OF THE STATE OF PLAY IN SOUTH VIET-NAM. YOU SHOULD KNOW THAT AT THE WSAG[1] MEETING TODAY THERE WAS ALMOST NO SUPPORT FOR THE EVACUATION OF VIETNAMESE AND FOR THE USE OF AMERICAN FORCE TO PROTECT ANY EVACUATION. THE SENTIMENT

OF OUR MILITARY, DOD AND CIA COLLEAGUES WAS TO
GET OUT FAST AND NOW. . . .

OUR TASK—YOURS AND MINE—IS TO PREVENT PANIC
BOTH IN SAIGON AND WASHINGTON, AND I KNOW THAT
YOU RECOGNIZE THIS MORE THAN ALMOST ANYONE IN
THE UNITED STATES GOVERNMENT. . . .

IT IS ESSENTIAL, DESPITE THE CONCERNS THAT YOU
HAVE EXPRESSED AND THAT I ACCEPT, FOR YOU TO
SPEED UP THE MOVEMENT OF AMERICAN CITIZENS OUT
OF VIET-NAM.[2]

The US government and I had just come to very different con-
clusions about a fundamental question: Should the Vietnamese
people who had helped Americans get our help in the event of
an evacuation? The American government said no. It was time, it
thought, to cut its losses and get out. I disagreed. As an American
and as an officer of FNCB, I felt morally bound to protect the safety
of the people who had worked with me for so many years. The next
day, I was on Air Vietnam's morning flight—its last flight—from
Hong Kong to Saigon.

John P. Riordan, United States Army, Captain, Studies and Observations Group, in Saigon, 1968.

FNCB's Saigon staff outside the bank for the branch opening, 1972.

Riordan and his boss, bank manager Michael J. McTighe, at a client reception, 1973.

Riordan at the bank, January 1975.

The calm before the storm.

Betty Tuyet, Secretary to the Bank Manager, at her desk.

(Top) Jim Eckes, Continental Air executive and CIA operative, the catalyst of the adoption plan.

(Center) The bank's advisor, Nguyen Thanh Hung, refused to leave, but his youngest son, Nam, left the country as Riordan's son.

(Right) Thirty-three-year-old Riordan claimed Tran Minh Ha's seventy-year-old mother, the oldest in the FNCB group, as his daughter on evacuation paperwork.

(Top) After the evacuation, the Saigon staff gathered outside the refugee tents at Camp Pendleton Marine Base, California, 1975.

(Center) Smiling faces on the Saigon staff thirty years after the Fall of Saigon at a reunion in 2005, Orange County, California. Chuyen Uong is first row, far left, the author is center of the first row kneeling next to Tran Minh Ha, Pham T. Cuc is second from left in the second row.

(Above) Three generations gathered at the most recent family reunion, 2013, at the Long Island, New York, home of Chi Vu's daughter. Chi is in the third row, center, smiling broadly.

CHAPTER 10

April 18, Return to Saigon

I WONDERED JUST HOW long it would take for my bosses in Hong Kong to realize I was gone. Bill Walker already knew. Early that morning, I had emptied my meager personal items into a bag, closed up my room on the fourteenth floor, and gone down to Walker's room on the twelfth floor, all before seven a.m.

"You're going back," Walker had said flatly when he saw me standing at the door. My knock had gotten Walker out of bed, and he was still in his shorts. I was dressed casually, in jeans and a button-down shirt—not my standard banking attire. I also carried a small travel satchel in my hand. One look at me and Walker knew what I was up to.

He had been at the meeting with me the day before. He had heard, as clearly as I had, the warning the regional managers had delivered. Bill looked at me with respect—and a bit of fear. He knew exactly what I was risking.

I didn't have time or inclination to explain, so I just asked him, outright, for all the cash he had so I could buy a ticket to Saigon. I tried to look confident, but it was a thin veneer. I was sabotaging any chance of a future career in banking, and going back to a place where we all knew hell could break loose at any minute. But Walker didn't try to stop me. Instead, he gave me all the cash he had, which was about two hundred US dollars. He handed it to me and gave me a firm handshake good-bye. "John, be careful," he said as I walked away.

The others would find out when I didn't show up for breakfast at the hotel. Someone from FNCB Hong Kong finally thought to check my room. When I didn't respond, they inquired at the hotel desk; they found out I had already checked out. "Is he crazy?" the FNCB Hong Kong people asked. When they checked the flight manifest for that Air Vietnam flight, Hong Kong to Saigon on Friday, April 18, it certainly seemed crazy. There was only one American name listed—mine.

Word of all this traveled quickly back to FNCB's Head Office in New York City. My sanity was the subject of hot debate in the executive dining room on the thirty-eighth floor of the Head Office. I know that in New York they put odds on it: bankers ate their lunch and got a cigar from the maître d', James, casually placing a bet on their way back to their offices about whether I would get out of Saigon and whether I would really be fired. But those who knew me vouched for me. They said that no, I was not crazy. It was assumed I had a plan.

I was hoping that one would come to me quickly.

On the surface, things in Saigon seemed not to have changed very much. That was puzzling to me rather than reassuring. I didn't know what to expect—maybe a city on lockdown, a shadow of itself. But cafés and restaurants were still open; noodle shops were still ladling out steaming bowls of soup to their customers, who ate, drank, and gossiped. The sidewalks were still packed with stalls offering an astounding variety of American goods: watches, whiskey, spare mechanical parts, and cigarettes. Open carts tangled with Saigon's cowboys on their motorcycles on the city's wide boulevards. These cowboys were young men who had somehow gotten draft deferments, through family connections or school. The daredevils traveled in packs around the city on shiny Japanese motorcycles. The cowboys were identifiable by their outfits, tight pants, and colorful shirts with rubber sandals on their feet. Presumably they were still bored enough to find dodging traffic thrilling. The city's loose habits were still on display. Bar girls lounged in the shade, and a horse race was held at Phu Lam near the airport. And yet, according to my briefing by Colonel Wahle at the DAO, the North Vietnamese Army was practically at the gates. He could be wrong, I supposed. Maybe the city wasn't going to fall to the Communists after all. Maybe all this fuss was for nothing.

Just under the usual bustle of the city was an underlying sense of restlessness. It was hard to define precisely what was giving me that impression. The masses of barbed wire and gun-toting South Vietnamese soldiers had been there as long as I had, as a soldier and as a businessman. But after my time in Hong Kong, maybe I was starting to see that Saigon was cut off from news about itself in a way the rest of the world wasn't. By April 18, the real facts were grim: Two-thirds of the country's land area was in enemy hands. Almost half the provincial capitals had been taken, and the North Vietnamese Army had just claimed the highway between Saigon and Vung Tau, cutting off Saigon's main access point to the sea.[1]

War had been an ongoing fact of life for the Vietnamese since World War II. After thirty years of conflict, most people, including me, thought that the end would be long and slow in coming. But in the last two months, one province after another had swiftly fallen to the North Vietnamese Army. The Communists were marching toward Saigon. Part of me kept thinking that the Americans would land at any minute to rescue the South Vietnamese. Well, I thought, if they plan to come, they had better come quick.

The South Vietnamese staff members of my bank were absolutely terrified that the North Vietnamese Army would get into Saigon before they could get out. The Communists had shown how cruelly they could crack down during the Tet Offensive in 1968. That uprising had ended in their military defeat, but it was still a bloodbath. Mass graves full of civilians had been left behind, full of mutilated women and children. It was feared that if the North Vietnamese Army got through to Saigon, this time the retribution would be much, much worse.

————————————

To my knowledge, the only time that I came face to face with the enemy had been when I was in the army. I had been on a high-speed boat, ripping through the choppy water of the South China Sea on my way to an island off the coast of Vietnam. I was going there to discuss the island's medical resupplying needs, but I shared the boat with a dozen prisoners and their guards. The men, handcuffed and silent, were on their way to some kind of interrogation and internment. I was told that they were the enemy, either Vietcong guerrillas or captured North Vietnamese soldiers. Studying them from a safe distance on the boat, I saw nothing at all to distinguish them from the Vietnamese guarding them with rifles or from the Vietnamese I was routinely surrounded by in my daily Saigon life.

Other than that, I had only seen the enemy from a thousand feet in the air. I can remember one of my first weeks in country, a young soldier had been manning the side door to the C-130 as a machine gunner. He was spraying bullets in a wide arc from the plane. During a momentary lull, I asked him, "What are you shooting at?"

"Those Vietcong," he replied acidly.

Looking down to the ground, I could see black-garbed figures running for cover in the tall grasses or flopping into the paddy water to escape the rain of bullets. "How can you tell if they are VC?" I pressed the gunman.

He replied without looking at me, still scanning the blurred countryside below: "They're wearing black pajamas!"

I was shocked, and then I got really mad. "All the farmers wear black pajamas here." This wasn't a western, with the good guys in white cowboy hats and the bad guys in black.

I yelled at the soldier to stop firing, but my protest was drowned in another outburst of machine gun fire. I made my way up to the pilot; he was in command. He heard me out, but the set of his jaw told me that he wasn't going to say anything. Everyone else on board was averting their eyes from me, and that suddenly scared me. I had heard that fragging was on the rise in Vietnam—unpopular commanders were being killed by their own soldiers. I wasn't about to further jeopardize my safety in Vietnam by making a scene or making enemies on my own side. After that, I kept my mouth shut.

Good guys or bad guys, Communists or imperialists, the lesson I took from the war was that nothing was ever clear in Vietnam. For the bank evacuation, I had been trying to come up with a list of staff members we should trust absolutely. There was a column for those I was afraid might have Communist sympathies and another column for those I suspected might be South Vietnamese loyalists—anyone who might see an evacuation plan as treason and report it. I knew Chuyen and Robert had their own lists, but as soon as I got back to Saigon and saw the emotional reaction to my return to the bank, I decided to throw my list away. Anyone who wanted to come could come. Now I just needed to find us a way out.

I arranged to meet Jim Eckes at twelve forty-five in the courtyard garden of a whitewashed concrete-and-brick apartment building just outside Saigon's District 1. It was lunchtime, so all the shades were drawn around us, but I don't remember eating. My nerves were too keyed up to stomach anything.

The apartment building opened up on the courtyard. A gecko trilled at my arrival. The horn of an occasional taxi echoed against the green walls, and the sounds of the *com rang* restaurant tucked into the alley were muffled. Eckes was already waiting for me. When he stepped out of the shade, he looked the same as he had at our meeting in the hotel room—he was even dressed the same, in tan pants and a short-sleeve, button-down shirt. The only difference was that his fair hair took on a reddish cast in the sunlight. I studied him intently. Was he trustworthy? I had checked with Pan Am and a few other airlines that did business in Saigon. No one seemed to know much about him. I simply had no other choice but to believe I could trust him.

Eckes came straight to the point: "The situation on the ground is changing faster than we can plan for."

"Can you still help us? I've come all the way back to Saigon . . . "

"Of course, of course." Eckes seemed surprised that I would ask such a question. Then he explained that the escape strategies that had worked for other clients the week before were no longer going to be feasible options for FNCB's staff.

I couldn't help asking, "What were you doing?"

One of Eckes's most reliable tactics had been simply to get plane tickets to other cities in South Vietnam. No exit visas or embassy stamps were needed for domestic travel. Once the Vietnamese were ticketed and inside the airport, Eckes's many contacts would help them avoid the immigration police and get to the international terminal. From there it was just a matter of slipping onto flights out of the country. "The problem," he explained, "is that there are no more flights to any other cities within South Vietnam. They've all fallen to the Communists."

As Eckes explained the problems he faced in getting our staff out, he wasn't chatty or warm, just factual. I found his forthrightness businesslike and reassuring. I didn't need a smooth sales guy right now; I needed a plan I could count on. "What can we do?" I asked Eckes.

"First thing is to get your people gathered together, grouped into one or two centralized locations, with as little fanfare as possible."

The bank's employees lived all over the city, many of them with family members beyond city limits. People had begun to speculate that the roads into the capital would be closed if things got bad enough. I don't know if anyone was deluded into thinking that closing the city limits would keep the Communists out, but at least it would slow the flow of people fleeing from other collapsing cities in South Vietnam. Refugees were already beginning to stream in; Saigon was like a sinking ship taking on water.

"Okay," I told Eckes. "My villa has plenty of room, and Bill Walker, our operations guy, is in Hong Kong. So his house is empty but still rented by the bank. We'll bring them to the two houses right away. What else?"

"Sit tight for now," he counseled. "The Americans are about to begin the evacuation. The Marines will arrive at Tan Son Nhut and secure the airport."

I must have looked confused. Jim thought it was about the evacuation logistics, but something else was bothering me. I was thinking back to my embassy-sponsored trip to Saigon—had it really been just four days ago? That printed list of 627,000 names I had seen spilling off the embassy staffers' desks bothered me. I hadn't actually seen any names, much less the names of our thirty-four staff members. "Jim, can you find out for me if in fact our employees are on that list?" I asked Eckes.

Jim shook his head. No list existed—not that he knew of, and he would have known.

As it turned out, a few months after the fall of Saigon, I would see those men from the embassy again. The same ones who had showed me the pages of Vietnamese names would come up together from Washington, DC, to call on me at FNCB's Head Office in New York City. They came specifically to apologize. They faced me and said, "We knew we were lying to you at that time, and we just wanted you to hear it from our lips."

Eckes was right; there was no list. The list the embassy had showed me was just for show.

"So are they, I mean are we, well—how exactly is the United States embassy planning on evacuating the South Vietnamese?" I asked.

Jim spoke carefully: "There is not going to be a general evacuation for the South Vietnamese. American aircraft will come in and evacuate the remaining American citizens and their immediate families." Jim drew out the word "families" and looked at me from under arched eyebrows.

I didn't understand. "Why are we going to be sitting around and waiting for the Americans to evacuate American citizens if everyone on my staff is South Vietnamese? What's our plan here, Jim?" I asked him.

"You will adopt them."

Colleagues as family: that was part of our corporate ethos at FNCB. McTighe and I had even told Eckes as much during our

Hong Kong meeting. We included husbands, wives, and children of our employees in our accounting. We had one husband and wife on staff, Bien in the audit department and Thoa in general ledgers, but I never could keep up with how many other different interconnections there were among the Vietnamese staff. Cuc's husband was best friends with Chi's brother. Chi and Hien were first cousins. Cuc's cousin was Chuyen's wife—or something. The South Vietnamese were gracious in including in their family traditions the Americans who had come to Saigon for work: they tried to make us feel at home by celebrating holidays together, inviting us to weddings and funerals. We hung together through good times and bad—and now I had just risked my job to come back for them.

So yes, okay, I could say that these people were my family. But how was I supposed to sell that to the South Vietnamese immigration officials? Or to the American government? Some of the staff were older than I was. I had seen ads in the papers from people looking to exchange family status as a ticket out: children were looking for adoptive parents; brides were looking for husbands. But everyone on my staff was too old to be an orphan, and almost all of the women were already married. *How many wives can I possibly have anyway?*, I wondered. In rural parts of Vietnam, there were different marriage arrangements, or so I understood.

I ran through the list of staff in my head. There were thirty-four South Vietnamese employees at the branch. Almost all of them were married, and many of them had kids. It was over one hundred people. Who would ever believe a crazy plan like that would work? Only a man who has no other options.

CHAPTER 11

April 19–20,
Weekend in Saigon

S OME OF THE VIETNAMESE confessed to me later that I was the last person they had expected to see back. McTighe was more likely, but they didn't know that he had been physically stopped from being able to return. The staff could have expected a bank liaison in Saigon, like someone from the lawyer's office, sent by the bank to help them out. I seemed young and ambitious, not at all impetuous. And I was analytical, so maybe the Vietnamese staff read me as being remote. I'm told that once people get to know me, I'm warm and folksy, but I suppose in Saigon, especially in the weeks leading up to the end, my softer side was not on display.

I was definitely not thought of as the kind of guy who would risk his job, and his life, to come back and help staff members he had only worked with for two years. Burning a million dollars, defying the US ambassador: these things were absolutely out of my character, I admit it. But the rush back to Saigon to help the staff seemed like a natural instinct to me. The only surprise was that to do so, I had defied the bank's direct order. But I guess you never know what will push someone to explore their limits.

Over the weekend, the staff began to move their things into Walker's old house and my villa. The houses were only a few blocks apart, and both had high walls surrounding the properties. It was somewhat reassuring to think that the sudden influx of so many people into the residences was concealed from easy view, but it was impossible to relax completely. Chuyen had told Cuc, who told everyone else. Cuc was young but had a fill-the-room personality. She was perfect for the personnel department because she was the kind of woman people listened to. The first step of our exit strategy was to get everyone to the centralized locations. Cuc communicated that order to the staff and told them they had better get there quickly and bring the minimum with them. One small bag each. No luggage, no obvious jewelry, nothing out of the ordinary. They should be dressed in their work clothes, and they should only carry as much on them as they might reasonably bring to work. It had to look natural.

On the fly, it was decided that the men should stay at Walker's house, and the women and children at my villa—even though my place had some touches that made it decidedly a bachelor pad. I had converted an old wooden teller's desk from Manila into a liquor cart full of bottles of Scotch and whiskey. But the French school across the street provided some cover for the sudden influx of women and children.

I decided it would be more appropriate for me to stay with the men at Walker's house rather than try to make myself unobtrusive among the women and children in my own home. Walker had left for Hong Kong with his wife and child in such a hurry that his two-story villa on Pham Ding Phung was still fully furnished and even had a small staff to run it. A cook and gardener helped the house's new occupants. A tall brick wall surrounded the property. The big gate was made of solid metal, so no one could see through it. Walker had told me that the villa had once belonged to Madame Nhu, the notorious, despised, and deposed First Lady of South Vietnam. In the summer of 1963, she had shocked the world when she called the Buddhist monks' suicides "a barbecue" and said she would clap her hands to see another one. Her family's regime was overthrown a few months later, and the former first lady was now in European exile.

Madame Nhu's tastes had run toward the opulent. In the presidential palace, she had a silk-upholstered bed and real tiger skins covering the parquet floor. The home Walker was living in was more modest, but in addition to two upstairs bedrooms and a kitchen, it also had a library and a great room. In other words, it was large and could accommodate a number of our people in comfort.

Wives didn't want to be separated from husbands, and vice versa, but no one ever complained to me. Everyone understood. In case of evacuation, the women and children would go first. It seemed the chivalrous thing to do, especially since the disastrous Danang evacuation just three weeks before was still fresh in our minds. Women, children, and old people had been left behind, along with anyone who had not been physically strong enough to battle for a spot on the tarmac and race against thousands for fewer than two hundred seats on the plane. The flight out of Danang had been full of able-bodied young men.

In our situation, women and children actually had a better chance of getting out. The men ran the risk of getting drafted if they weren't already conscripted into service, or of being shot on the spot for desertion or treason. There was a real fear that some disgruntled South Vietnamese soldier assigned to guarding the exits would shoot first and ask questions later.

FNCB had a disproportionate number of women on staff. The imbalance was due to the fact that most South Vietnamese men were working in some capacity for the military or the government. Most of the men who moved into Walker's house that weekend were not bank employees, but the husbands of people on our staff, which meant that we had high-ranking officers in the army and government officials in our crew. I passed no judgments. I knew how hard it was for these men to say good-bye to their country. Were they supposed to sacrifice their families too? It was not for me to say who should and should not be leaving. If anything, these men had the most to fear from a Communist victory.

As Walker's house filled with men, the mood grew increasingly tense. I could see that they were nervous about their wives and children: there was a lot of pacing the floors and smoking. I wasn't about to lock anyone inside the house, but I did try to remind everyone that too much movement in and out would arouse suspicion. Many of the men were not bank employees and did not speak English. I relied on Chuyen to communicate for me, but he was especially preoccupied and cranky that weekend. He had practical concerns on his mind. "I still have a bank to run," Chuyen grumbled. "And you keep talking about taking out my employees."

I stopped whatever I had been doing and stared at Chuyen. He couldn't be serious, could he? To my mind the bank was functioning in Saigon for show only. I had stopped working on any real bank-related business before I left Hong Kong, and besides, I was fired. My focus was solely on getting people out of Saigon.

"To be honest, Chuyen, I don't care if the bank is running or not right now," I growled.

Chuyen took personal offense. My disregard for bank business was disrespectful, and that was grounds for an argument.

"Wriston himself told me that I am in charge of this branch," he said. He raised his voice, which quivered with barely concealed anger. "We cannot just shut down. People will panic; clients will demand their money. It will cause problems for the company, and tell me, how will we handle that?"

I took a deep breath and forced myself to think about it from Chuyen's point of view. He had done a fine job of running the bank branch in Saigon. Wriston had personally sent a telex saying that he entrusted the branch to Chuyen, who should be congratulated on doing a great job so far. Before signing off, Wriston had made sure to reference the fact that they were "fellow alumni"; both Wriston and Chuyen had graduated from the Fletcher School of Law and Diplomacy at Tufts University. It was such a thoughtful and personalized telex, and it came directly from one of the most esteemed and powerful men ever to run a financial firm. Chuyen had tacked it up for the whole staff to see on the branch's bulletin board. In all the chaos to come, it was the one thing that Chuyen would regret leaving behind. When the Communists eventually did storm through the city, the telex would still be on display.

Chuyen had run away from North Vietnam as a teenager and been in the South Vietnamese Army for nine years. He had a diploma in politics from an elite American university and had even worked at the American embassy in Saigon for a while. Now he was a high-ranking officer in a capitalist bank. Chuyen's résumé encapsulated everything the Communists were against. If he were taken into custody, who could guess the amount of "reeducation" it would take to break him? As he voiced his very real concerns about running the bank, I realized that this was not a man worried about his safety. Chuyen was so loyal to FNCB that in spite of significant danger to himself, he was still worried about the company.

As a bank we had promised to protect our clients' assets, and our sizable reputation was on the line for that. So I could see what Chuyen was thinking. Things in Saigon were still so calm. It just didn't seem possible that the Communists were less than a hundred miles away. A city about to fall under siege was supposed to be chaotic. But where were the looters and explosions? What if the country didn't fall? We had to have a plan for every eventuality.

My only defense was that I had seen the memo. Wriston had reiterated that the staff's safety was paramount. I read that to mean that the bank's assets were secondary. "Look, Chuyen, Wriston told you that no matter what you do with the bank, the safety of our staff is what is most important," I gently reminded him. "Let's get people into place to go, and keep just enough to cover our asses at the bank, okay?"

So far, there had only been one issue with winding down the bank's operations. One of the bank's better-known customers was a woman who ran a large fruit plantation in the delta. She often brought ripe papayas and pineapples as gifts for the staff to enjoy on their breaks. She was an elegant woman, easy with a smile and wealthy from the look of her well-cut pantsuit and jade jewelry.

"I've received this letter from the bank," she had said, pulling out a typed letter on FNCB stationary to show Hien, a customer service representative. The letter had been written to certain bank clients to inform them that FNCB was immediately refunding their prime deposits. Prime deposits were made for fixed periods of time, ranging anywhere from six to thirty-six months. The variable interest rate was guaranteed up front and linked to the prime lending rate, so if the prime rate changed, the client benefited.

Hien calmly explained to her customer that FNCB Saigon could no longer guarantee future payments. "We will return your money to you in cash," she began, but the woman cut her off by shaking her head.

"I don't want to take my money out. What if I refuse to accept it?" challenged the woman. "I have no place to put that much cash. What else am I going to do with it besides keep it in the bank?"

The plantation owner's tone remained pleasant the whole time, but it was clear there was no room for discussion. This was a woman accustomed to getting her way. Holding her head high, the woman turned on her heel and walked out the door.

The rest of the weekend, waiting at Walker's, felt interminable. Eckes had nothing to tell me except to keep waiting. Cuc in the personnel department made up a list; Chuyen, Robert, and I went over the numbers again and again.

Of the thirty-four Vietnamese employees at the branch, thirty-two were coming with us. One young woman, a teller on the main banking floor named Nguyen Khoa Thuy Diem, had another way out. Her father worked for an American news organization—I think it was *Time* or *Newsweek*—and it was organizing its employees' evacuation. So that was one person we didn't have to worry about.

Nguyen Thi Than from the bookkeeping department on the second floor had also told us that she wouldn't come with us, but in her case, it was because she was forbidden. Chuyen called Than's father several times over the weekend: "Please, allow your daughter to come with us. She will have a job in the United States; she can send for you." But Chuyen's pleas were ignored. Than's father was immovable. As it turned out, Than would leave the country anyway. She fled as a "boat person," five years after the fall of Saigon. She was one of the lucky ones: she made it to the United States alive.

"So I've got thirty-two Vietnamese employees to adopt, plus their families," I read from my notes, looking up at Robert and Chuyen for assurance.

Robert shook his head. "You will have thirty-one. I have a Taiwanese passport that I can use to get out."

"Why are you still here?" I wondered aloud.

"My wife," Robert answered factually. "She cannot travel on the passport with me. Will you still take her with the others?" he asked. Of course, I assured him. But I had real concerns. Even without the two women and without Robert, our group was still huge. I had only a rough estimate of how many children everyone had and whose husband or wife was coming, but by my reckoning, I had over one hundred people to get out of Saigon—and fast.

What difference would a few more make? Over the weekend, while I waited for Eckes to give me a signal, I thought I might try to convince a few of the bank's most trusted Vietnamese advisors to come with us.

Advisor Nguyen Thanh Hung had been a consultant for FNCB since we had commenced operations in Vietnam, and the staff always referred to him formally, as "Advisor." He was older than anyone else in the bank, in his mid-sixties, and he had had a long and distinguished career in banking. Prior to becoming a consultant for us, he had been the inspector general of all the banks in Vietnam. Advisor Hung had been invaluable in giving FNCB advice on how to work in Saigon, and with whom to do business. I couldn't imagine trying to leave without him.

I drove out to the advisor's house in Ben Hoa. Hung lived about fifteen miles out of the city. I didn't know how to get there, so I had my friend Bich with me. He was the bank's lawyer, and he knew Hung. As it turned out, I would be glad I hadn't gone alone.

"Advisor Hung, would you and your family come with us?" I began to ask, but was cut off when Advisor Hung lunged at me and grabbed me by the collar of my shirt.

"Goddamn you Americans! You caused this horrible mess."

The man's black eyes were absolutely wild. I was taller than he by six inches or more, but he had stretched up and, in a flash, wrapped both his hands around my neck. I was so surprised I didn't move until he began to squeeze, choking me. I gagged. Bich pried us apart. I took a few steps back, trying to regain my breath and find a way out. But before I could say anything, Hung lowered his gaze and apologized in a tight voice.

"My family will stay. My father is still living." The tradition of filial piety was too strong for Advisor Hung to break. His father was eighty-nine years old, and Hung could not bring himself to leave his elderly father to face the Communists; the family had already run away from them once. In the early 1950s they had fled North Vietnam to take refuge in Laos and Cambodia before making a new life in Saigon. "But my youngest son, Nam, would you take him with you?" Hung beseeched me.

"Consider it done," I vowed. I could not blame Advisor Hung for his emotional outburst. I would be feeling the same if I found myself in his shoes. If he wanted to give his youngest child a chance at freedom, of course I would help. "Just get him to Walker's villa by this weekend." The eighteen-year-old was traveling by himself to make a life in a new country without his family. The poor boy looked bewildered when his father dropped him off, and he came with only the shirt on his back. I told him to go upstairs to my closet to take whatever he found that might fit him.

As it turned out, Advisor Hung's father didn't live long. He died just two months after the fall of Saigon. By then, it was too late. Hung, his wife, and the rest of their children were stuck in Vietnam. The new regime got word of Advisor Hung's experience in banking, and they put him to good use. The Communists recruited him to help them nationalize the banks. But after six months, the Marxist economists decided that this old man was a capitalist relic and no longer relevant. Advisor Hung was retired from banking and sent to be reeducated in a labor camp. It was years of physical toil and grueling work. He got out in 1981, just in time to see his wife before she died of an aneurism. The son Hung asked me to evacuate, Nam, would eventually become an American citizen in 1990. He was able to sponsor his father and a sister to come to the United States in 1992, but Advisor Hung was old and sick by then. He lost both legs to untreated diabetes and died in 2008.

Hung wasn't the only one I failed to convince to join the bank evacuation. Dr. Uong Ngoc Thach was another one. The doctor had saved me once. I was terribly sick with a kidney stone attack shortly after I arrived in Saigon. I was convinced I was dying. Thach soothed me with medicine and spent the night in my villa checking on me. I've followed the doctor's advice and eaten a bowl of high-fiber cereal every morning since, and I've never had a kidney stone again. Dr. Thach earned my undying devotion, and I thought it might be my turn to pay him back for his kindness by helping evacuate him. Dr. Thach appreciated my offer, but he didn't want my help getting out. He was prepared.

"I won't go," he said stoically. "I was on the other side; I know how they are."

By "the other side," Thach meant he had been either Vietcong or Viet Minh, the Vietcong's precursor. He had left the Communists, and he knew just how bad their retribution would be. All the more reason, I argued, he should come with me.

But Thach refused, saying, "I will take the Black Pill rather than face them again."

I also asked two of the bank's lawyers, Bich and Kinh, if they would come with us. They worked for a shrewd and intelligent woman named Madame Trai. She had already gotten out and was in

Paris by the end of April 1975. Bich and Kinh, Madame Trai's junior associates, had been left trying to hold the firm together. Through my time at the bank, both of them had become my close friends.

When I asked, Kinh insisted he was going to be fine. Caltex, a subsidiary of Chevron and an important client, had promised him a way out. When we reconnected years later, Kinh had moved to Texas after the fall of Saigon.

The other lawyer, Bich, declined for family reasons.

"My old mother and my two young sisters—I have to take care of them," he told me. "I will be fine."

After a while, he actually was fine. But first the Harvard-trained lawyer had to go to reeducation camp to undo all his capitalist learning. It took six years. After a thorough reeducation, Bich got a job as an advisor to the new government's Ministry of Oil. When I went back to Saigon (renamed Ho Chi Minh City) in 2010, he was doing very well for himself. Bich sent a car to fetch me and my partner from our hotel in the city. The driver drove us to a large home outside of the city. Bich's wife fixed us a delicious lunch, and we reminisced pleasantly for a while before Bich finally asked, "How come you never asked me to go with you?" Poor Bich had been reeducated so completely that he had no memory of my offer.

———————

On Sunday I made the short drive from Walker's house to my villa. I wanted to see how the women and children were settling in. The moment I opened the door, it was as if I had stepped into a madhouse. Someone flew by in a flash and thundered up the stairs without seeing me, and I could hear a teenage girl hollering after a laughing gaggle of kids in the yard. Their mothers had formed a circle near the kitchen, cackling and gossiping while they peeled the skin off small fruits they tossed carelessly on a growing pile. The shades were down, darkening the room and making it seem even more stifling. I only had one air conditioner, up in my bedroom, and relied on ceiling fans for the living room. All they did was push the stagnant air around. There were papers everywhere, laundry drying on the back of furniture, stacks of dishes in the sink, and the sharp smell of stale garlic and fish sauce.

I had grown to love Vietnamese food, and I could appreciate the complex flavor that fish sauce lent to the national cuisine. The Vietnamese call it *nuoc mam*, and they put it on everything. The condiment is as ubiquitous in Vietnam as ketchup is in America. It's made from fish buried in salt until it ferments. When the smelly liquid drips off, it is bottled and sold. The complex flavor of *nuoc mam* is one thing, but there is no getting used to the smell. I didn't appreciate the odor of fish guts permeating my place.

"What the hell is going on in here?" I asked, but no one heard me. I picked my way around the mess, getting madder and madder with every step. I have always been pretty fastidious about picking up after myself, and it was physically uncomfortable for me to see my well-tended home in so much disarray. Bedrolls, pillows, and blankets were tangled in corners. Furniture was upended to make room for so many people. Every available surface in the kitchen was covered with food preparation items. I knew it was temporary—the result of so many people living in a tight space—but it was also dangerous. They had not even noticed I was walking around. It was loud with talking, crying, and laughing. It was advertising to the whole world that something unusual was going on. I couldn't hold my temper another second. All my pent-up anxiety over the restless weekend, the frustration at so many failed attempts, all came roaring out of me.

"SHUT UP!" I yelled.

Heads finally turned toward the front door. Everything got quiet except for the wail of a child upstairs, but even that was quickly shushed. No one at the bank had ever seen me lose it before, and they stared up at me as if I were some horrible monster. I was red-faced, and my eyes were bulging out of their sockets.

"I want these kids QUIET. And I want this place picked up. I'll be back in one hour."

I turned on my heel and tried to leave gracefully but ran into a chair that wasn't supposed to be there. I shoved it out of the way with my foot and huffed out the door.

When I got back, it was three hours later. I had calmed down but was still worried that my people were being so careless. We had to keep a low profile. My background in the clandestine service (SOG) made me nervous about making our presence too obvious. I had heard that police searches were becoming a relatively routine occurrence in Saigon. They would be ostensibly looking for deserters, but "outsiders"—anyone staying in a house who was not registered at that address—were also rounded up. Maybe a bribe would suffice, maybe not. I did not intend to find out, and I needed to explain the situation to the women in my villa, but perhaps a bit more reasonably. When I got back to the house, the place was spotless. Total peace and quiet greeted me when the front door opened. I heard footsteps squeak upstairs and a worried face poke down the staircase, but I grinned.

"That's better," I said politely, "please keep it this way."

CHAPTER 12

April 21,
Breaking Curfew, Saigon

"HELLO, JOHN. Topping here." The voice of the Pan Am director in Saigon boomed over the phone at Walker's villa. "Welcome back to Saigon!" We both had a quick laugh at that. Topping had heard, possibly from Eckes himself, that I was back to help FNCB's staff.

"I've got a plane, a regular Pan Am flight, coming in tomorrow. I've got a bad feeling that time really is running out. I'm getting some of my own people out on that plane."

"What about exit visas? Or immigration papers?" I probed.

"Don't have 'em." Topping admitted he was just banking on the situation getting chaotic enough that a few people at a time could slip out without the proper documentation.

"Bring ten people out to the airport on Monday at five p.m. I'll get 'em round-trip tickets from Saigon to Hong Kong."

I jumped at the chance. This sounded way better to me than an adoption. Ten people were a fraction of the total we were trying to get out, but every bit helped. Besides, if the plan worked, maybe there would be more flights. Topping's flight was completely above board as a regularly scheduled flight. It would just be a matter of sneaking people on. With help inside the airport, how hard could that be? I was fully aware that the departure of any of my South Vietnamese staff had still not been sanctioned by their government, or mine, but it had the blessing of Pan Am. Topping made no secret of the fact that it was a risky plan. "It's kind of a test, but we want to try it. You've got to think about who should go."

Chuyen and Robert helped me decide on the ten people to ticket for the Pan Am flight. It was arbitrary, and I can't remember whom we chose, only that everyone else went to work on Monday to appease Chuyen. I don't remember what the women were wearing or how many children there were, only that there were two families, and we all fit into the bank's van. I was sitting in the front seat.

The whole thing was surreal. I hadn't quite believed it when Topping had said that our tickets would get us through any barricades, but sure enough, he was right. The tickets got us through the police checkpoints. The military also waved us through. No one but people who were really able to leave the country had tickets from Pan Am, I supposed. When we got to the airport, we settled into the waiting room, and for a moment I relaxed.

Then I looked out on the tarmac.

We had a perfect view of the 747 from the waiting room, so it was impossible not to notice the flurry of activity surrounding the plane. Men in blue uniforms were like ants crawling around the whole thing. They were on the wings of the plane and looking down inside the windows. They crawled around the underbelly as well and even looked into the wheel wells. It seemed to me there were dozens. I had never seen dark blue uniforms on officials in South

Vietnam before; everyone was usually in white or grey or khaki. So these men must have been airport customs, but the sight of them was jarring.

Al Topping strode over to me in the waiting room and said, "John, I need to speak with you."

"Of course, Al," I replied casually, but I followed him a few paces away from the rest of the group. A sour taste was rising up my throat; I knew it was going to be bad news.

"It's not gonna work, John," said Topping. "You can see them out there. The immigration police are all over this plane." Al looked upset, but not nearly as stricken as the faces of the families from FNCB that I could see behind him, staring at us from where they sat in plastic chairs. Two women had started to cry quietly into their handkerchiefs.

"I'm sorry to do this, but I am going to have a real hard time even getting any of mine on that plane." Al sighed, leaving it understood but unsaid that it was hopeless for anyone who was not a Pan Am employee. "Go on home."

Tamping down my own rising cry of disappointment, I turned to face my group. I forced myself to meet their eyes and whispered a few words of banal encouragement—something to the effect of, "We'll try again," although I wasn't altogether sure what it was we were going to try. The eleven of us, the FNCB group of ten plus me, backed out of there and drove into Saigon.

We returned to Walker's villa from the airport just in time to watch the news. It was grim. The South Vietnamese president, Nguyen Van Thieu, had resigned that afternoon. I wasn't surprised; after all, Thieu had violated his own decree, "Never retreat." It had been five weeks since the fall of Ban Me Thuot, a town in the Central Highlands, and this was the political blowback. As it turned out, Thieu himself had ordered the South Vietnamese Army to stand down, abandoning the Central Highlands to the Communists. It still felt strange to watch Thieu break down so publicly. He had been the president for long enough that his tenure stretched from before the first time I came to South Vietnam as a soldier. Thieu had won the presidency in 1967 and again, in elections widely described as fraudulent, in 1971. He didn't seem to be terribly popular among the South Vietnamese people. The *New York Times* would sum up the Thieu I remembered in a few lines in his 2001 obituary: He was "not a prepossessing leader. His manner was not dramatic. His speeches tended to be long, rambling, dreary and often incoherent." Still, Thieu had been endorsed by America so long it seemed a telling sign that he was finally crumbling.

Thieu took to the national South Vietnamese airwaves—radio and television—on Monday night. He started in the late afternoon, but by the time he was done, it was dark outside. Thieu cried on live television and then railed against the United States for more than an hour. Thieu said that his forces had failed to stop the Vietcong because of a lack of funding from the Americans. He also suggested Kissinger had tricked him into signing the 1973 Paris Peace Accords, and then Thieu called the US military cowards. "You Americans with your 500,000 soldiers in Vietnam! You were not defeated. . . . You ran away!" Afterwards, the vice president, Tran Van Huong, took over the presidency in a small ceremony. The seventy-one-year-old asthmatic was leaning on a cane but vowed to fight on for South Vietnam, "until all the troops are dead or the country is lost."[1]

Thieu's resignation was met with tears by many of the staff. It wasn't that he was so well loved. For many of the people at FNCB, Thieu's resignation was the first time they realized that the upheaval all around them was outside of the normal chaos and meant something. This evacuation might not be so temporary after all.

The resignation jolted me into a state of alertness. Finally, something was happening. "This is it," I thought. "The evacuation is beginning tonight!" Eckes would surely try to get in touch. I ran through a checklist in my mind. All the men were at Walker's, the women at my villa. We had warned everyone that it might be a quick departure. They were supposed to be ready to go, but something nagged at me. Were we really ready to go? I felt a pang of guilt when I thought about the bank. The vault was full: there were piasters and dollars in there, along with travelers' checks. If we left those behind, we would be risking assets of FNCB.

I wasn't supposed to care anymore. I wasn't on the payroll. But maybe something Chuyen had said over the weekend had inspired me. He had been so determined to see things through with the Saigon branch. Or maybe I was still a banker at heart. Whatever it was, I found I just couldn't leave knowing the branch had cash and travelers' checks, not to mention the codebook and Simplex date-stamp slugs—not in good conscience. We had to get it all out of there.

I easily talked Chuyen and Huy into going with me, plus Bien in the audit department. Quynh and Hai came with us too; I didn't know them as well, but we all understood what we had to do. We got in the white Mercedes, and I sped from Walker's house to the bank. We had to get there fast, not just because Eckes could call at any moment, but because Thieu's resignation and the presidential handover had prompted a stricter curfew in Saigon. This one was to last from dusk to dawn. I supposed a little leeway might be granted this first night of the curfew, and apparently I wasn't the only one. Vietnamese dashed every which way, trying to do the things they had to do before the new curfew was enforced. From here on out, no one was supposed to be out on the streets of Saigon after dark.

It took us less than ten minutes to get to the bank. I drove down the wrong side of the street, but traffic rules in Saigon were always somewhat arbitrary. I parallel parked right in front of the bank entrance—still facing the wrong direction, but I was grateful for the open spot. I shut off the engine and lights.

"Open the door," I called to one of the Pakistanis guarding the door. He looked half asleep but startled to life when he recognized me banging away on the glass. He opened the door without a word or a moment's hesitation.

"Thanks," I called behind me. Chuyen and Huy followed closely as I made my way to the bank's vault.

We grabbed stacks of cash. The rest was in travelers' checks. The money and checks got stuffed into large army duffel bags that closed with a heavy-duty zipper. It was awkward to carry, and the stacks of money shifted around in the bag. We took everything that was left in the bank vault. If I had to guess, we probably took over $200,000 in travelers' checks and $10,000 in piasters, but the exchange rate was inflating so rapidly that the total value of the piasters might have decreased by half in the roughly ten minutes it took us to drive from the bank back to Walker's villa. Chuyen carried our branch's copy of the FNCB codebook, which broke down any sensitive banking or personnel words into something mundane like "Tree," "Cloud," and "Cracker" for transmission on the telex. Before leaving, I had the presence of mind to grab the Simplex date-stamp slugs. Those were what we used to validate deposit slips and record entries into safety deposit boxes. If we left the date-stamp slugs behind, someone might try to make a false claim. I was caught up in the spirit of the heist, taking anything I could carry, so I made a grab for the primary books and records, but Chuyen stopped me. "Leave those behind," he told me. Chuyen was right. Those documents would be the only way the national bank could continue to wind down operations, pay depositors, and collect any loans. I left them in plain sight on the desk for someone to find, and we ran out with our duffel bags past the guards.

"Close it up behind us," I called to the guards. I had a fleeting thought for their safety, but they had Pakistani passports, so they would be fine. "Yes, sir, Mr. Riordan," I heard before the steel shutters came clattering down over the main door. While Chuyen and Huy stashed the two duffels in the trunk of the car, I got back into the driver's seat, breathing heavily from the exertion and anxiety. I called to the others, "If the police show up here and see us taking all this money out of the bank, they're going to arrest us!" The excitement of the night put a teenager's smile on my face as we raced back to Walker's house with all the money. We had just robbed our own bank! If the police had caught us, it would have been a complicated situation. It wasn't what I wanted to explain.

Back at Walker's villa, the adrenaline wore off. I began to fret. We had the money, but what were we going to do with it? The national bank was closed and at this point might never reopen. How could we get our assets into the right hands? Chuyen and I turned the matter over every which way. The Vietnamese currency would be burned, we decided, since the piaster wasn't worth much anymore. More important were the travelers' checks, and we would simply have to try to take those with us. FNCB would be on the hook for them if they were left behind and used, no matter who used them.

With a sinking feeling, I realized how little I had thought it all through. I had cash and checks that didn't belong to me. No matter how good my motives were, I was now a thief. I was about to adopt 106 members of other people's families. What kind of half-baked plan was that? What if I got in trouble? What if this perjury was punishable? But as rational as I tried to be, I couldn't see any other good answers. I comforted myself with the thought that at the very least, I had done what I could to keep my friends, and the money, out of the enemy's hands. If it failed and came crashing down around me, at least I had tried.

I needn't have worried. No call from Eckes ever came. No announcement of evacuation, no buses to pick us up for the airport. I wasn't adopting anyone that night. Eventually, I put myself to bed.

The sun rose, and morning came. It seemed impossible to me, but April 22 was going to be just another Tuesday morning after all. I brushed my teeth and got dressed. I was taking my time getting ready to go to work, but then I remembered the bank's empty coffers. The thought of the trouble we might cause if the loss were discovered shook me into quick action. "My God, Chuyen, we have got to get to the bank!" We had to put all the money back before anyone noticed.

CHAPTER 13

April 22, Day One

I WASN'T THE ONLY American left in Saigon, but our numbers were shrinking fast. Washington was putting pressure on Ambassador Martin to draw down the number of American citizens left in South Vietnam to the number that could be taken out on one helicopter. I didn't know of any American businessmen who were left, but there were plenty of others: journalists, missionaries, and do-gooders with voluntary aid organizations.

Air force planes had been landing in Saigon with increased frequency. On paper, they were dropping off military cargo to support the South Vietnamese, but in fact they were increasingly being used as a way to help American citizens, third-country nationals, and precleared select Vietnamese out of the country. It was not advertised as an evacuation, but nonessential Americans were told to leave Saigon from the Defense Attaché's Office (DAO) at Tan Son Nhut. The planes were not going out full, even though there were, in theory, lots of Americans who needed to get out. Lines grew to a mile or more, with people waiting for more than twenty-four hours, because of passenger processing and immigration checks. Vulnerable American planes were sitting on the ground and then taking off nearly empty. By April 19, only six thousand evacuees had flown out of South Vietnam on military flights.[1]

People like me were staying back to help their South Vietnamese friends and colleagues, but we weren't the real problem. There were a large number of American contractors, most of them former military, who had hired on with the US Mission or the South Vietnamese government to perform specialized tasks—building roads, working on telecom, repairing helicopters. Those men had spent enough time in Vietnam to think that the current fuss over recent Communist victories was just another storm that would blow over. Many of them had made a life for themselves in Vietnam: they had married Vietnamese women and had children, or adopted the children of common-law wives. They were in no hurry to leave.

Ambassador Martin's disdain for these men broke through his usually formal speech. He used a sexual slang to refer to contractors who married Vietnamese women, calling them "lotus-eaters."[2] Whatever he thought of them personally, it was Martin's job to make sure that all American citizens in South Vietnam departed safely. The only way those men were going to leave Vietnam was if provisions were made for their new Vietnamese families to follow them.

That was lucky for me, and Eckes knew it. The US Justice Department had handed the State Department the authority to "parole" certain Vietnamese into the United States. They were giving great leeway to the definition of family, all in an attempt to convince the stubborn American contractors that it was a good time to repatriate. An American principal—someone to vouch for members of their Vietnamese family—was still needed. But "principal" became synonymous with "sponsor," and that was anyone responsible for cost of transportation, care, maintenance, and resettlement.[3]

Major General Homer Smith, commander of the DAO, realized the potential in the new provisions. Despite the intimidating language used by the Immigration and Naturalization Service, this was the ticket for getting large numbers of people out of South Vietnam. Smith told his boss, Ambassador Martin, that with their new authority to parole Vietnamese, and this broad provision for family members, "any American in Saigon could get out just about anyone he wanted to." They would just have to fill out a form he invented on the spot, something he called the "affidavit of support." It sounded just bureaucratic enough to make it official.[4]

Eckes called me at the bank on Tuesday morning. This was the moment we had been waiting for, he explained. He gave me a stack of prestamped forms; all I had to do was fill them out and sign them. That would be enough to adopt everyone in my bank group—including employees and their immediate family members—totaling 106 Vietnamese people.

Here's what the form said:

> I John P Riordan, an American Citizen, Passport number D 203902, hereby certify that the following named persons are my dependents and that I will assume all financial responsibility for their travel and resettlement costs.

On each form there was room for fifteen names, single-spaced, along with their nationality and a column in which to state the relationship between the principal and the dependents. This was where I was to write that I had one wife, seven daughters, and seven sons. The witness line was stamped and signed; all that was needed was my own signature and an address. Since I didn't have a current US address, I used my parents' on West Coyle Avenue in Chicago. I could just imagine their faces if these fifteen women and children showed up on their doorstep claiming to be my wife and children.

141

I am not a person who enters into agreements lightly, but Eckes made it clear that this was not only the best chance we would get but probably our last card to play. I was too caught up in the paperwork and distracted by the magnitude of what I was about to do. I did not inform anyone I was adopting them until after it was already done.

Family ties are a big deal in Vietnam. The family is the basic social unit of society and the cornerstone of Vietnamese tradition and religion. Allegiance to the family is the fundamental principle of Confucianism: filial piety. With one piece of bureaucratic paperwork I was going to upend generations of traditional lineage. I just wasn't sure how seriously people would take it.

One thing my experience in Asia had taught me was the importance of hierarchy. The form of address in Vietnam was entirely based on one person's relationship to other members of the group—what you called them changed based on age, gender, or even whether that person was (rhetorically speaking) from your mother's side or your father's side. Perhaps no other culture puts as much thought into how people relate to each other, but if everyone was already referring to everyone else as family members, like older brother, maternal aunt, or nephew, I thought, what difference would a mass adoption make?

I had no time to waste on worry. Perhaps the traditional Confucian structure of Vietnamese families had already gone to my head. If I were adopting all these people, then this was a patriarchal family, and by that reasoning, I was going to be head of the household. My responsibility was for the group, and my foremost consideration was their safety. I was not going to worry too much about how they individually felt about being adopted by me, even though some of them were older than I. So they would find out later. As it would turn out, leaving South Vietnam and moving to a brand new country was so disorienting that the adoption was taken with a smile and in stride.

Nguyen Thi Ngoc-Dung was a typist at the branch. She was a beautiful young woman with big black eyes. I hadn't had the chance to know her well—she was one of the last staff members hired at the bank. On Tuesday afternoon, she timidly approached me.

"If it is not too late, Mr. Riordan, can you please add my husband to the list?" Dung asked.

"Of course, Dung," I said distractedly. "We've said that we can evacuate immediate family members." As I spoke, I realized I hadn't known Dung was married. She was on Cuc's list as single. "Dung, I'm so sorry. I didn't realize you were married."

She smiled a sweet smile. "It's recent," she said. I felt awkward, but I had to ask her for proof. The irony did not escape me: I was the last person who should be judging the legality of family relationships. But I couldn't afford to make an exception and risk the entire operation. Before I had the chance to bring up looking at the paperwork, Dung said, "I have a copy of the marriage certificate with me."

She handed it to me, and I glanced at it. The piece of paper had the registrar's seal, and it looked official enough to me. "Congratulations," I said sincerely. "I'll look forward to meeting him. Bring him to Walker's villa tonight." *My first daughter to be married*, I thought.

After the evacuation, I would find out that Dung and Minh had gotten married just a few hours before she approached me. Usually getting a marriage license in Saigon took two weeks. Minh worked at Saigon University as a professor of animal science. He was in no real danger, but he had no desire to live under the Communists. And besides, he loved Dung. If she stayed, it could be bad for her as the employee of an American bank. If they were going to stay together, Minh and Dung realized that they had to get married—and quickly. They bribed their way through the system to get the registrar to approve a rushed marriage. They paid a cyclo driver waiting outside the town hall to be their official witness. Within thirty minutes it was done. They celebrated their wedding by sharing a glass of iced sugar cane juice on the side of the road, and their marriage lasted thirty-four years, until Dung passed away from liver cancer.

I did make two exceptions to the rules. First it was for Betty, my secretary. She had been engaged to a kind man named Andy. I knew they were planning on getting married, and I would vouch for them if I had to. The second exception was for Tran Minh Ha's husband. He was a captain in the South Vietnamese Navy and had left on a mission up the coast. Before leaving, he had told Ha that she should take any opportunity the bank might give her to leave with their young daughter. He assured her that he would find a way out of the country and not to worry about him. Since we had already counted Ha as part of a couple, she asked if we might let her mother go in her husband's place. Ha was her only child, and Ha couldn't imagine leaving her mother behind. I relented and made plans for the mother to go.

On the night of what would be the first of several successive trips to the airport, Ha showed up with her husband on Walker's doorstep. "His ship has been sent to the navy yard for overhaul," Ha sobbed. Her husband had counted on commandeering the boat out of Vietnamese waters if the Communists came, but with the ship now being serviced in the yard, that plan had been squashed.

To be honest, I had forgotten all about the swapping out of Ha's immediate family members. I had told Ha that I would take her mother in her husband's place, but I couldn't very well go back and dismiss a seventy-year-old woman while taking her only child away. I couldn't be the cause of Ha leaving her husband behind, either.

"Stay with me, here. It's the safest place for you," I said to Ha's husband.

Ha wailed. Their daughter, her mother, and Ha would leave first. Maybe she was afraid I would not follow through on my end of the agreement. Ha grabbed my arm, crying hard: "Please, promise me that you will try to help my husband get out of Vietnam!"

I looked at Ha sternly. Crying was dangerous. We had no lights on, and everything was supposed to be quiet. People were supposed to be calm. I summoned a severe voice, one I hadn't known I could manage. "I am risking my own life to stay here. I will try my best, but I am not God. I don't know how long I can stay here, but yes, Ha, I will try."

Ha bit her lip and said good-bye to her husband, hurrying in the falling dusk to be back at my villa with the other women before curfew.

She told me later that waiting for news of her husband had been like sitting on burning coals. But she hadn't complained again.

We couldn't all go to the airport at once, not if I had any hope that someone would believe I was the father of so many children. We would have to leave in small groups—a few at a time so as not to arouse suspicion. But there was still one problem: we needed to keep the bank running as a cover. By evacuating women and children first, we would be emptying the ranks of the staff before we could get everyone out. We had mostly women on staff to run the day-to-day activities at the bank, and most of their husbands were not FNCB employees. Our only solution, we decided, was to employ the men at the bank. When the wives left, the husbands would fill their jobs. Military men and government officials would be standing behind the tellers' counter and making change. But it would just be a short while, we reasoned. Things were bound to even out; the ship would tilt one way or another. If things in Saigon stabilized, the women would come back, the bank would still be running, and we could pick up where we left off. If things got worse, everyone was in position, ready to go.

I still had the unused tickets from Pan Am. Eckes thought I might as well have them on me when I went to the airport. I hoped that no one would be examining anything too closely. I had ten tickets for a flight that had departed the previous day and adoption papers for fifteen women and children I was not in fact related to. But we were desperate, and it was time to try something. We crammed into the bank's van, a blue GM rally wagon with a sliding door on the passenger side. We affectionately called it the Blue Goose. I sat in the front seat as Hanh, the bank's driver, expertly navigated through the crush of traffic leading to the airport.

We were just one of a long queue of cars and taxis waiting to get through the gates of the Defense Attaché's Office (DAO). The DAO was where I had met with Colonel Wahle for his gloomy report just the week before. Then, the road to get in had been nothing like this. Road etiquette had always been lax in Vietnam; it wasn't uncommon for traffic to block lanes. But that day I noticed that almost no one was fighting it on the other side of the road coming into the city.

There was a collective holding of breath as we finally worked our way up to the gate. I was anxious that security coming in would be tight. But as soon as I flashed the pack of Pan Am tickets at the uniformed guard, he waved us through. As I looked in the rearview mirror with a reassuring smile, my eyes met those of Chuyen's wife. She was holding their two-and-a-half-year-old son, gripping him tightly in her lap. Chuyen had insisted that they be part of this first run. He thought it might inspire more confidence among the staff if Chuyen let his wife and child go along with this crazy plan.

I was glad for Chuyen's vote of confidence. I was feeling anything but. The moment I pulled through those grey gates of the DAO, I played visions of death in my head. *I don't feel good about this at all*, I said to myself. *I know my life is going to end one day, but I'd sure hate to be shot at an airport.*

My morbid thoughts may have been due to the fact that the DAO was on the same side of the airport as the morgue. I remembered that fact from my days in the service. In 1968, I had been on a task force assigned to think about issuing dog tags for our people in SOG, the clandestine Studies and Observations Group. Casualties had ticked up significantly that year, and because of the covert nature of our group, the morgue had been slow to ID the bodies. Part of my job was to take a tour of the facility. I remember thinking that the place was like a factory. It had fifteen-foot ceilings and unpolished cement floors. Forklifts crisscrossed the floor to move inventory, but instead of lumber or boxes, it was naked bodies of dead GIs shrouded in clear plastic bags before being stacked up. They were already embalmed and were just waiting for aluminum caskets before they could finish being processed, locked up, and shipped out.

The most awful sight, though, was on the cluster of a dozen tables in the middle of the room. The tables looked as if they were covered in shit. When I asked, I was told that they were in fact pieces of human remains, possibly ours, that the team was still trying to identify.

Seven years later it was a different human mess laid out for display on the tables at the DAO. There were piles of paperwork and stamp pads in front of harried-looking embassy workers who didn't seem thrilled to have been pressed into service processing immigration claims. I joined a line in the gymnasium after dropping the fifteen women and children at the tennis courts. I was happy to get away from the courts. They had high wire fencing surrounding them

147

and teemed with humanity. There was a musky smell of so many people mingled with the scent of food being served from a nearby hangar, whose overhang was the only shade. Greasy food wrappers floated like tumbleweed among ratty suitcases and wicker baskets. Tired children clung limply to their mothers. It was damned hot.

"Stay in line. Keep your papers out for examination," bellowed a military police every few minutes. It looked like embassy staffers were processing papers while marines and air force personnel were in charge of keeping lines moving. Whether they were easing anxiety by providing protection or making it worse by their armed presence was anyone's guess. Thankfully the long lines of people waiting were moving fast.

The first clerk I came to looked at the list of names on my paperwork and then up at me. With a smirk he said, "My! You've got quite a family here, haven't you?" He clucked under his breath, but he stamped the form anyway. I turned my handwritten names over to someone who typed them up. Then I shuffled to the next table, where I was given evacuation number tags for each name on the list. That was it.

I did not have to answer a single question. Except for the wisecrack from the first clerk, the other staffers had barely glanced at my passport. I gathered up the papers and went to join my fourteen new children and my wife to wait at the tennis courts for our flight to be called. I couldn't quite believe we were clear.

My eyes kept darting around the perimeter of the waiting area. It was so crowded and, despite the barbed wire surrounding the compound, so vulnerable. One incoming mortar round and we would be flattened. I could hear the occasional rocket whine in the countryside or the dull thwack of big explosions far away, but I wasn't sure which side the noises were coming from. A few South Vietnamese fighter planes still screamed out to patrol the countryside, and helicopters flew low overhead. The military presence was not wholly reassuring. All it would take was a few disgruntled South Vietnamese military types to decide the departing Americans were going to pay for their mistakes, and the DAO was the perfect target. I was sure that gray-and-white-uniformed policemen were going to make their way through the barbed wire at any moment. Or that the ants who had swarmed the Pan Am plane the previous day would come poking through our paperwork.

My secretary, Betty, told me later that she saw her brother as she was getting on the plane. He was one of the military policemen in charge of keeping order. Betty was part of a big family, and she was torn apart by leaving her parents, four brothers, and three sisters behind. She cried for the fact that her brother was one of so many young men doing his duty while she was leaving the country. She wouldn't see her family again for another twenty years.

As I was waiting at the airport among the crowd, my eye settled on a priest. It had been years since my last confession, and I had been far from what was considered a good Catholic for a long time. But the sight of him walking out of the canteen stirred something inside me. He was tall, thin, and bald. I would find out later that he was Father Joe Turner from Philadelphia and that he was at the airport escorting orphans, ranging in age from four days to ten years old. I intercepted his walk timidly. "Excuse me, Father," I inquired carefully. "Could I have a word with you privately?"

He smiled in agreement and walked with me across the green cement to the side of the courts. With the encouragement of his kind gaze, I explained that I was with FNCB Saigon and trying to help over one hundred people to evacuate South Vietnam. As I spoke, my fears came rushing out of me.

"I've got all these people to take care of, and I just want to make sure they get on that plane. I think I had better go with them, because, well, I said I would be responsible. But what if I can't get another flight back in before time runs out? I've got so many others, other groups that are waiting for me to adopt them."

I was worried that I had said too much. I was exploiting a loophole in the immigration code to adopt so many people, and the Bible was clear on deceit being a sin. But the priest's eyes brightened at my story. Father Turner was on my side. "Hell, your group is already on the tennis courts," he remarked. "Don't worry about a thing. Since they are here already, they are going to get on those planes. They are in the system." Father Turner braced my arm reassuringly, but when he spoke, his advice was issued in an urgent tone: "Go back and get that next group."

CHAPTER 14

April 23–24,
Days Two and Three

I WENT BACK AND FORTH to the airport five times on Wednesday. And five more on Thursday. Each time I brought groups of 6, 8, or 9 with me. I didn't want to press my luck and try 15 again, but I had 106 people to get out. There was no time to waste.

The flow of cargo planes in and out of Saigon continued. Forty flights a day were landing and departing, around the clock, which meant that every half hour or so the deafening roar of another plane taking off or landing would roll over the DAO compound. I got so used to the sound that I didn't even hear them anymore, but the sight of them taking off into the sky was still amazing. These cargo planes were such huge hulking things that getting them off the ground seemed an engineering miracle in itself. Lockheed called the C-130s "Hercules" after the strongman in Greek mythology. They were built to be workhorses, and in Vietnam they had already seen plenty of action. The C-130 turned into a gunship with the simple addition of a cannon and side-firing weapons to the fuselage portals, or a bomber if you rolled explosive canisters out the ramp. It sprayed herbicide and dropped flammables, but its main use in Vietnam (until this point) had been to resupply isolated forward bases with food, bullets, and troop reinforcements. Now these C-130s, along with C-141s, were the fastest and surest way out of the country.[1]

The cargo planes were not what anyone would call good-looking planes. Neither type was authorized to take more than one hundred passengers, but as many people were crammed in as would fit—two hundred, sometimes more. An American in uniform sat on sand-bags near the plane. He used a bullhorn to call out names. His pro-nunciation was not very good. In fact, the Vietnamese later admitted to me they never could understand if their names had been called at all. A garbled sound would come out of the amplifier, and one family after another would present themselves. You had to be quick and assertive, or you would wait forever.

Hien, one of the women I helped, told me later that the jostling for a spot was so hectic, someone stepped on her shoe, causing it to break. She didn't have time to try to find the broken half, so she left South Vietnam half barefoot. Getting a proper pair of shoes was Hien's first request at the evacuation center. When she was handed an eleven-year-old girl's hand-me-downs, she was so grateful she wept. Another evacuee, Lien, remembers how hot and thirsty her three children were while waiting on the tennis courts for their names to be called. There was a military tanker truck full of wa-ter for the Vietnamese, but no cups. Lien rooted through a growing pile of trash, finally finding an empty Coke can. She rinsed out the syrupy residue and used it as a water receptacle for her three little boys. I had only ever known Hien and Lien as well-dressed, pro-fessional, and modern young women. It was shocking to think that one left South Vietnam barefoot and the other scavenged trash for something to serve as a water cup. Desperation had remade these women into refugees.

The planes took out hundreds at a time, but the crowds and the lines just kept getting bigger as the days progressed. On Tuesday, the fifteen FNCB employees, spouses, and children had been part of a total of three thousand evacuees who flew out of Saigon that day. Five days later, twelve thousand flew out. No one could guess if or when the Communists might lose their patience and target the airport, putting an end to the fixed-wing evacuations.[2]

At least the bureaucrats had shortened the process so that people could be moved along relatively quickly. When I had come with the paperwork for the first group, they had taken my handwritten list, and someone had typed it up. By the next day, they just accepted my names written in longhand. I could only have one wife, so I listed everyone else as either my son or my daughter. I didn't get too creative. For a brief time, the in-laws of American men with Vietnamese wives had been allowed out, and then abruptly, the rule was narrowed to immediate family only. People were informed of the rule change by a fellow with a bullhorn. All around me people were furiously scratching out changes in their paperwork, from mother-in-law to mother, from sister-in-law to sister. I was just as happy to keep it simple. If these people were going to be my family, they might as well be my children.

I was still working off the list prepared by Cuc in our personnel department. She knew who was married and who had children, how many and what ages. We decided to get the families with children out first, single women next, and the men after that. Not everyone was happy with that plan.

Can was the husband of Xuan, who worked in our bank's credit department. He worked for one of the national banks, and he did not have an escape route any other way, yet he did not think it was safe for her to go alone. He asked her to stay. Xuan felt she couldn't disobey her husband's wishes, and I had a hard time accepting that. I told her, "I came here to evacuate you, but if you don't follow my instructions, you are going to be left on your own!" I had always thought of Xuan as a modern, progressive woman. Maybe I got that impression from her wedding pictures. She had worn an American-style, white wedding dress with a veil, even though the traditional color for weddings in Vietnam was red. I got Tony Bui to call Xuan's husband. Xuan and Tony worked together, and, coincidentally, their respective spouses worked together at the National Bank of Vietnam. So they knew each other a little.

I listened as Tony made the call. He spoke in rapid Vietnamese, which I made no attempt to follow, but the gist of it was that while Tony admitted he was scared too, he was more scared of the consequences—facing the Communists—if they stayed. It took Tony a while. They were on the phone nearly a quarter of an hour while I hovered nearby. Finally, Tony convinced Can that if they were to be good husbands, they had no other choice. Can relented, and as it turned out, the men became close friends after the evacuation.

When Tony's own wife, Loan, was loaded into the van, she looked panic-stricken to be without her husband. It was such an emotional time; all around her were crying children, and women who already knew each other were chattering away. Tony took a gold ring from his finger and put it on his wife, saying, "In case you need the money, sell it." Tony's wife spoke no English at all, so I was at a loss to reassure her, but I did sympathize. She was leaving her life, her family, and her husband behind to get into a van with a bunch of strangers. They were her husband's colleagues, not hers, and they were all leaving the country, even though their destination was not immediately clear. She could only hope that Tony would be able to follow before it was too late. Tony and his wife had been married a little over a year, and they had no children yet.

Tony would join her soon, I tried to explain, but I was careful not to make any promises. I intended to get everyone out, but there was no guarantee of anything. She looked at me blankly; she couldn't understand a word I was saying. Tony himself was leaning against the van, conferring with Lien.

"Please look after my wife," Tony was asking Lien. "She cannot speak English, and it is the first time we are going to be apart." Lien had three young boys, and she was leaving the country alone, without her husband, since he was still flying F-15s around the falling country. Tony knew the last thing he needed was to put an extra burden on Lien, so he made a deal with her. If she would help look after his wife, his wife would help with the three boys. In thanks, Tony and his wife would name Lien as the godmother of their child.

I recognized how hard it was for families to separate—husbands from wives, children from their fathers. I did my best to make everyone understand that it was for their own safety. I was doing what I thought was best. But on Wednesday afternoon I made a mistake. I separated a mother from her children.

I was getting ready to make my fourth round-trip to the airport, my last for the day, when I called out for Chi, our bank's head teller. She had six children. They had been at my house for several days, waiting for just this moment. But when I called for Chi, she didn't respond. Her children were there; I saw them huddled together with Hien. Hien was Chi's twenty-five-year-old cousin who also worked at FNCB, in the bank's customer service department. She looked down at the floor when I asked her where Chi was—no one was supposed to leave the villa. "She went to go get food for the children," another woman called out from across the room. "They were so hungry."

I wasn't at all mad, just focused on the fact that it was past time to get the rest of the kids out of here. What if Chi got hurt and couldn't get back? Would I risk the children's safety to reunite them with their mother? I had to make a decision fast. The other group that was supposed to be in this fourth run to the airport was a group of four young children, and their mother was heavily pregnant with the fifth. The youngest of Chi's kids looked about four, and the oldest boy was fourteen. If the Communists did come, fourteen was old enough for him to be conscripted into the North Vietnamese Army. That decided it. Getting these children out of South Vietnam safely was my priority at that moment. Their mother would catch up to them, and besides, they had their cousin with them.

"Miss Hien, how about you?" I asked. "Will you take the children?"

Looking back on it now, I didn't realize what I was asking her to do: asking a single young woman to take responsibility for her cousin's six kids, and take them to—well, no one knew where exactly. The planes were going to either Guam or Clark Air Force Base in the Philippines. Both seemed a universe away from Saigon, but going to either place was safer than staying. I can still hear the hysterical sobbing that wracked poor Chi when she came to my house and found her six children gone.

"Where were you?" I asked her. "Why weren't you here?"

Chi couldn't tell me. Many years later, Chi finally explained. Her time of the month had surprised her that day. She couldn't imagine staying in my house, possibly having to evacuate in such a state. So Chi had rushed home to bathe and grab a change of clothes, plus any feminine products she might need for the trip. But by the time she got to my house on Wednesday night, her children were gone. I tried to console her, but nothing would quiet her sobbing until I told her I would take her and another group too, despite the curfew.

As it turned out, Chi's plane would go to Guam, the same place where her children's plane had gone. It would take them an impossibly long day in the camps to find each other, but in the end, they did.

The American officials at the processing center in the DAO gymnasium either didn't realize that I was processing four dozen dependents in a day, or didn't care. As far as I know, I only raised eyebrows twice. Once was in response to the first group I got out—the clerk's snide comment about the size of my family. Consequently, I hadn't dared again to create groups exceeding nine family members. The second time was when another American official in the processing line said to me on the second or third day, "You look very familiar." I thought that was probably going to be it for me, surely the game was up, but to my great relief, he just smiled and passed me on.

The trips to the airport never became routine. Traffic in Saigon was always harrowing. My worry about the driving risks probably came right behind my worry about a rocket attack or VC sabotage. People simply did not stay in their lanes. There was no concept of people who were moving in the same direction staying on the same side of the street. Instead, there was always a level of traffic chaos. It would become a real problem when a train went by. Halfway out on the main road to Tan Son Nhut were heavily trafficked railroad tracks. When a train came through, the barricade would go down, and all the traffic, cars, cyclos, scooters, and carts would pile up in a mass on one side. When the barricade finally lifted, the two massed sides faced off against each other, like a card deck in the hands of an unskilled shuffler.

Hanh, the bank's driver, drove the van, and I always sat in front. The ride from the city probably took fifteen to twenty minutes. For the last mile or two, I would ask half the people in the back of the wagon to lie low. I handed out the unused Pan Am tickets to the other half for them to flash when we approached the airport gate,

157

just in case the MP stopped us, which only happened twice. He took just a cursory look inside.

I don't want it to sound as if I were relaxing into this experience, because I wasn't. Every muscle was twitching; all my senses were attuned to what might be dangerous. It made my usual easygoing manner downright surly.

Cuc was one of the last women to leave. She had a two-and-a-half-year-old son, her husband was in the military, and her father had been a high-ranking official in the South Vietnamese government before his retirement. On Wednesday, when I finally called Cuc's name for a spot in the van, the normally composed and professional Cuc refused. "I can't go," she said. "What if I never see my husband again?"

"Cuc, come to your senses," I pleaded with her.

But Cuc wouldn't listen. "My husband can manage; we only have one child; he is not heavy," I realized Cuc was not saying she was staying in Saigon, but that she thought she might leave a different way than I was offering. She was thinking about running.

Cuc had momentarily lost her mind. She thought that there would be other chances for her and her family. She couldn't see what was right in front of her. There were so many stories of people fleeing and dropping their babies or dropping dead of exhaustion that Cuc had begun picturing the evacuation as a test of strength, like a mountain that had to be scaled.

"How will you get out?" I probed gently.

"By boat or helicopter" was the matter-of-fact answer. Someone else took her spot in the van on Wednesday, and by Thursday it seemed Cuc had regained her mind. But once she was in the van and on the way to the airport with her baby son on her lap, she completely lost it again. She began to sob in the backseat. "I am leaving my family—I didn't get to say good-bye. And my country! I am

homesick already!" The wailing got louder and louder until I finally turned halfway around in my seat and roared at her: "Goddamn it, Cuc! You have got to cut it out. Or else I am going to have to kick you out of this van."

She looked at me with huge eyes, but at least she stopped crying.

"You can't be carrying on like this. People are going to think I am kidnapping you. You are making this dangerous for everyone."

My outburst at Cuc may have been what prompted another member of our group that day, Mai, to remember me as a character as gruff as Rooster Cogburn. John Wayne played the one-eyed marshall in the western *True Grit*. I had to say I was a bit flattered by the comparison. Rooster had been stripped of his badge because of questionable behavior, just as I had been fired by the bank for disobedience. Rooster had earned his way back through good deeds; I was too busy to care whether or not the bank wanted me back at that point. But if I had a moment to stop and think, I am sure I would have hoped there might still be a chance for me with the bank.

Cuc sniffed a few times, but she finally got a hold of herself. "I will do my best to make sure your husband gets out," I assured her, mellowing at the sight of her anxiety. Cuc nodded and stared out the window the rest of the way.

In theory, every Vietnamese going to the airport still had to have papers from the Minister of the Interior. It wasn't strictly enforced. Out of the thousands of evacuees streaming in, MPs would select maybe a dozen a day to send to the ministry for validation. Basically it was just enough to keep the officials there busy during the day. The officials would then push some papers around and stamp a few things in brightly colored inks, but eventually they issued the visas. The Americans had given those South Vietnamese officials their absolute assurance that eventually they would get out, along with their families. So the men wielding so much power with their red stamps were not inclined to hold up the process too much.[3]

We had one brush with trouble outside the airport gates. Bac Kien's son was in the van on Wednesday afternoon. He was just seventeen years old and still in school, but technically he had reached draft age. The guard looked at the boy for what seemed like too long of a time. Kien smoothly reached out and took the MP's hand through the open window. Kien said something under his breath, and there was a handshake. To this day, I still have no idea if Kien slipped something into the MP's palm, but the guard stepped back and lifted the barricade. Hanh hurried the van through the gates.

———————————

During all this, the bank was still open for business, but the staff was thin. The people who worked upstairs were recruited to come downstairs, and some of the spouses had stepped in. These were people who had never handled big amounts of cash, or clients, all of which made Chuyen very nervous. Wednesday morning, the staff got to work only to find a large crowd of customers already waiting for the doors to open. As soon as they did, people rushed in, asking to withdraw money from their accounts. The bank was so understaffed that it was a mess. A junior auditor from the second floor was asked for 50,000 piasters, and he handed the customer a brick of cash. A brick was two times the size of an actual brick and ten times the amount the client had asked for. The customer was an honest man and returned the whole wad of 500,000 piasters. By that time, the auditor was so flustered by the enormity of his mistake that he took the whole brick back to his desk, leaving the anxious customer to exclaim, "I am still waiting for my money!" The auditor finally got it right on his end, but it would take us a while to reconcile the books for those final days.

No one knew exactly what was going on. We were all winging it. The staff would be told that they were only going to work until noon, and then noon would come around, and people were told they had to stay until closing. If they were told to go home, just as they got there, they were told to report to my house. It was a terribly confusing couple of days, but people kept their wits about them. Everyone was moving in the same direction.

By Thursday afternoon, there were only a few male FNCB employees left holding the bank together with the help of several employees' spouses. It was getting impossible to keep up the appearance of business as usual, so I was grateful when the American embassy finally notified us that they were ready to help us evacuate our staff.

The embassy had no idea that so many of FNCB's employees were already out, or on their way out. By that point, I had gotten out ninety-three people. I had a dozen or so left, all men. This last group was the group I was most worried about because the husbands of several FNCB employees were in it. These men were either in the military or subject to the call of the military. Going out in public for them might mean getting caught for desertion—a very serious offense.

A team of US Marines had landed in Saigon to oversee the final withdrawal. We were really getting to the end. Vietnamese employees of American companies were directed to bring their immediate families to an intersection of a central Saigon neighborhood. I took the seven husbands of my staff members instead. The area was very residential—calm and quiet. I had never been through it before. There were nice houses around and pretty trees but no security. Hundreds of other people had shown up. They were local staff from Bank of America and Chase, as well as Esso and Caltex.

Idling nearby were a dozen buses with Vietnamese drivers. They were painted a military color, a deep army green, but I didn't know which army they belonged to. I had assumed that since the embassy had organized this assembly, it would provide protection. But before we boarded the buses, an American coordinator spoke for two minutes in impeccable Vietnamese. When he was done, a bumpy murmur rumbled through the crowd. As it was eventually translated to me, he had said, *"Chet! Chet!* Careful! Careful! All of you are draft age."* At that point in the war, the government was so desperate for manpower that the draft age for any male was between seventeen and forty-two. "We've just heard that the chief of police and security has been arrested and jailed for attempting to leave the country. If you are arrested, don't say I haven't warned you!" Everyone in the crowd already knew that the penalty for desertion at that time was death by firing squad.

It was dangerous, but at this point, everything was. I tried to talk the seven spouses of the FNCB staff into getting on the bus: "Come on, let's go. Let's take our chances here." But four of the men panicked. "It is too risky," they told me. All four were active military men. I couldn't blame them, but I was out of ideas. I couldn't promise them anything else would be safer. "I'll do my best to come back for you. Wait for me at Walker's villa," I instructed. "If you don't see me back late tonight, or tomorrow, you will know that I am stuck somewhere and can't help you anymore. Then it's up to you to take care of yourselves." I didn't mean to scare them, but I didn't want them to sit around and wait for me if I did get stuck or decided it was too dangerous to continue. Then I sat back down on the bus and rode with the three others who decided to take their chances.

I was the only American on that bus, and I sat up near the front, a few rows behind the driver. The others sat low in their seats toward the back. When the bus started moving, a Vietnamese woman who might have worked for Bank of America asked people on board to contribute money for the police at the checkpoint. Her timing was perfect. At the Vietnamese police checkpoint a few miles from the airport, a police officer boarded the bus asking for the list of passengers.

Like the other members of the National Police of South Vietnam, he wore a white cap and grey uniform. The getups earned the police the nickname the White Mice. But mice still have teeth.

"The list is short. Why are there so many people on this bus?" the policeman barked. The woman who had gathered the money showed him a clipboard. There was nothing pinned to it, but the clipboard served as cover for the pile of money she shoved toward him. The woman acted as if nothing were amiss. She spoke respectfully and courteously: "Sir, I am sure you will find that the numbers of people match the list." The policeman made a show of counting people and then turned around and said, "Alright! You are OK!" He signaled the guard to raise the gate, and the bus was allowed to proceed to the airport. The exchange rate of piasters to dollars was so high at that point, 755 officially and 6,000 on the black market, that she couldn't possibly have handed him very much money in such a small pile. But it was enough. The three men who came with me on the embassy bus to the airport were soon safe inside the DAO.

I had to admit to myself that I was tempted to stay with them. I finally felt that things were getting close to the end. Would this be my last chance to get out of there? I had not made any promises to the people at the bank that I would be back. All I had said was that I would do my best. But I couldn't stop now; I was so close. I caught a taxi and headed back into Saigon.

CHAPTER 15

April 25, Day Four

S INCE THE BANK'S DRIVER, Mr. Hanh, was safely at the evacuation site, I was now the driver of the bank's van. I figured it would take me two more trips to the DAO compound to get out the four husbands of FNCB staff and the six remaining male employees, and then I quickly added one more. I did not intend to forget myself.

But I was going to need help. The remaining husbands of FNCB employees were starting to get scared. They mentioned that someone suspicious had been hanging around the gate to Walker's villa. Maybe the men were just being paranoid, but maybe not. The important thing was that these men felt that there might be agents of the South Vietnamese government watching the house. Every one of these men was in the military. If they were caught, they would be imprisoned, maybe killed. Our CIA man, Eckes, was the only one I could think of to help.

"Alright," he said when I asked him, "I will go with you this time."

The military husbands and I drove to the airport on Friday morning in the blue van. No one spoke; everyone was nervous, thinking about possible outcomes and consequences. Chi's husband, Van, ran the biggest risk. He was a lieutenant colonel in the air force. Since Van was usually stationed at Tan Son Nhut, he was afraid he would be easily recognized.

We spotted Eckes's car a mile from the police checkpoint. He drove a little yellow Volkswagen, the last thing I would have expected from a spy, which might have been exactly the point. We pulled over for a quick rendezvous, and Van got out to ride with Eckes. When we started up again, I kept the van's nose to the Volkswagen's rear. Eckes must have had some contacts in the police force because as soon as his car appeared, the barricades all went up. He parted those checkpoints as if he were Moses.

We drove right out to the tennis courts. We were almost home free.

Since the bank had opened for business in Saigon in 1972, FNCB had the lucrative contract of doing the cash run for the embassy employees. Every other Friday the blue bank van would bring $1 million in cash for payroll to the DAO at Tan Son Nhut. With the official exchange rate hovering around 500 piasters to the dollar, four or five duffel bags were required to hold that much money. The dimensions of the bag were three or four feet by two feet, all of them stuffed full. You had to hold them closed with a rope. By the end of my time in Saigon, the piaster had devalued so much that it was 6,000 to the dollar. Our bank made money off the foreign exchange rate, so it was a profitable deal for us, and carrying that much money around always had an element of adventure. The Vietnamese had kept French banking codes, which meant that bank officers delivering the goods were licensed to carry a gun. It was usually the operations guys who went.

I had never had much luck with guns. I was issued a .45 to carry while I was in the service. I never needed it, and frankly, it never occurred to me to actually try to use it. One time, my commanding officer ribbed me about it: "Have you ever fired that thing?" When I said no, he told me to fire into the trash pit. I tried, and tried again, but that gun jammed on every round. I had to manually clear it, which was cumbersome and took time. The enemy would have overrun me and butchered me in the time it took me to clear the jam. I threw it into a footlocker and never carried it again, except to turn it in when I left Vietnam in 1969.

No one at FNCB had weapons during those last days in April 1975, at least not so far as I knew. But someone came up with a brilliant idea of using the bank run as a cover for getting into the DAO. It made perfect sense. We still needed to empty the bank vault, and we could pretend that we were taking the cash that was used for salaries to the DAO. Under normal conditions, the DAO would give FNCB a $1 million check in exchange for all the cash. The police would hang around and wait for us to take our check to the National Bank and deposit it. But this time, it was a one-way trip.

There were six men on FNCB's staff who came with me on the last bank run: Chuyen, Huy, Tony, Quynh, Hai, and Bien. We took the last dollars and piasters out of the bank vault on Friday. We broke all the Simplex date-stamp slugs, and then we waited until the lunch hour arrived. All the paperwork had already been destroyed. The only thing we forgot was Wriston's letter to Chuyen. (It was still tacked up on the employee bulletin board when we left, congratulating him on being in charge of FNCB's Saigon branch and requesting that he put the staff's safety above all other considerations.) We left FNCB at noon and asked the guards to pull down the gates as if we were closing for lunch—except those gates would never open for business again.

Our typical biweekly runs were under a police escort. We saw no reason why this should look any different, so Chuyen called for our usual assistance. One jeep drove in front of the van, and one behind. We had at least six policemen armed with automatic rifles, and their sirens were blaring. We drove right through the checkpoints to the DAO office.

Ann Hazard was the DAO's civilian chief disbursing officer. She was the one who usually called the bank to tell us when it was time to make a cash run. Since she didn't call this one in, she must have known, as soon as she saw us, what we were up to.

Ann had been in the civil service for twenty-six years but had never been under as much pressure as the last week in April 1975. Her South Vietnamese employees begged her for favors, or dollars, but Ann was a firm woman who played by the rules. She finally requested that a marine be posted outside her office door.[1]

US Marines with machine guns and automatic rifles were indeed stationed outside and around the building, but once we got inside, I saw no more guards. Ann was down a long corridor, and she must have gotten scared when she heard our footsteps rushing down the hall. It was the first time I saw her with a pistol in her hands. It stopped us dead in our tracks.

Her arm relaxed by her side as soon as she saw it was me, but I noticed that she didn't put down the gun.

"We've got cash in our duffel bags," I said, and started to explain that it was much less than the usual run, but Ann cut me off. "Just throw it in the room over there," she said. There was no paperwork to sign, and I didn't see any bookkeeping. Who knows how much Vietnamese and American currency Ann had been receiving those last days? When we walked in to drop off what was left in our vault, my jaw dropped. It looked like the Federal Reserve Bank of New York in there. Stacks of counted and tied dollars lay in towering stacks all over the place. This was payroll money and government funds, and none of it was going to get used. I knew it was headed for some kind of burn pile. It would have been so easy to grab a handful, but none of us did. We were more concerned with getting a spot on a plane than with money.

After the evacuation, Ann would be the subject of an official investigation into the disappearance of millions of dollars. She was eventually absolved of any wrongdoing, but the inquiry ruined her career anyway. The three and a half million dollars I saw in that room, along with eighty-five million in Vietnamese currency, was supposed to be destroyed. Ann was responsible for getting the cash placed in a fifty-five-gallon steel drum along with some kind of lighter fluid. But the barrels themselves were wired to the only communication satellite, the last tie from Saigon to President Gerald Ford and Secretary of State Henry Kissinger. So the DAO commander ordered a hold. It would blow up when the last Americans left—the whole DAO complex was wired for destruction.

But the barrels didn't burn. Aerial pictures of the DAO compound taken from thirty thousand feet after the American departure showed the DAO buildings and the satellite transmitter had been melted with thermite. For whatever reason, the barrels of money were still there. Ann Hazard was charged with "loss of funds" and then cleared, but for the rest of her life she would have to answer the same question: "What did you do with the money?"[2]

Greater wealth lay just a few miles away. The country's gold supply was stored in the Central Bank near the Saigon River. The State Department was supposed to help arrange for insurance that would cover transferring the gold out of the country, to Geneva or the Federal Reserve of New York. But the situation in Saigon had deteriorated too fast. By the time a policy was in place—insuring $60 million of gold when there was in fact twice that much—Thieu had resigned, and no South Vietnamese would take responsibility for the transfer. The gold remained at the Central Bank for the Communists to claim. It was already crated and ready for shipping.[3]

—————————

Once I dropped the bags of money, I turned to Ann and told her the real reason we were at the DAO that day. This was no ordinary cash run, and we all knew it. "I need to get these guys over to the evacuations area."

Ann was gracious and kind. "Go around to gate B, and tell 'em I sent you."

Just then, one of the FNCB officers who had been outside came running up to me. "The police guards wanna know if we'll take them with us too."

So the police knew what was happening at that point. Thankfully, they had already put their rifles down, and it didn't seem as if they wanted to stop us, but just join us.

I had my hands full, so I answered matter-of-factly. "Tell 'em we just can't."

I got back in the van and drove with the FNCB staff by a back road to gate B. There were a few American men in plainclothes and some marines.

"Ann Hazard sent us. These guys"—I jerked my thumb back to indicate Chuyen and the other Vietnamese—"are with me."

"Oh, no. They can't go. You can't take these guys out of the country, and anyway, who are you?"

I mustered all the bravado I could, and told him I was with FNCB. Then I barked, "Get Ann Hazard on that phone."

After quick words were exchanged, the American in plainclothes said, "Okay, Ann," into the receiver. He hung up the phone and raised the gate, and we were in. The last of the FNCB staff were on the tennis courts. I booked them, and myself, spots on an evacuation flight scheduled for a five a.m. departure the next day.

I had the entire staff and their immediate families taken care of. They were either at the DAO waiting on a flight or, I assumed, safely evacuated to somewhere in Guam or the Philippines. Besides the lawyers Nguyen Ngoc Bich and Nguyen Kinh, and Dr. Uong Ngoc Thach, there was one more person I felt I should try to get out. Nguyen Dich

Tuan was a Saigon police lieutenant. He lived twenty minutes away from the airport, and even if I could not get him to join the evacuation with me, I wanted to at least say good-bye. Tuan and I played tennis together at the Cercle Sportif. I could never beat him in tennis, but we were nearly evenly matched in chess. I would eventually win our late night matches by playing very slowly. Sometime around one or two in the morning, he would get impatient and make mistakes.

Tuan didn't hesitate when I asked him if he, along with his wife and their young child, wanted to leave with our group. He answered emphatically, "Yes, okay, of course, I'd like to leave." But there was one condition: "We have to get my parents' permission."

Tuan's wife was quiet on the drive to see her husband's parents. I had met her a few times and always found her sweet and charming, but Tuan had told me that she had a fiery side to her. I had seen it spark one night when our chess game ran a little too late. Tuan's wife had stood outside my villa, yelling for her husband to stop playing his game and get home.

During the whole ride to Tuan's family's house to ask their permission, she stayed quiet. She never mentioned asking her own parents, and I wondered if she at all resented having to do what her in-laws commanded. But I supposed that was the way things were done. I drove with Tuan, his wife, and the baby to the grandparents' house and waited outside for the three of them to say their good-byes. I didn't wait long. Tuan came out crying, followed by his grey-faced wife holding their child.

"They won't give me permission to go," he explained. "They say they've seen Saigon fall before. I must obey tradition. We have to stay." Tuan was in his late twenties, and to my American way of thinking, he should have told his parents to butt out. It was his life, after all—his to live as he saw fit, and it was his wife and child he needed to look out for.

As it would turn out, some members of my staff had feared meeting the same resistance from their parents. One woman at the bank lived with her mother-in-law. She was sure that the old woman would never let them go. So instead of asking permission, she lied. She used some excuse about the bank needing all employees to help collect special documents; it was something that could only be taken care of by bank employees, so her mother-in-law should not expect her home for a few days and nights. To my knowledge, that was the last time they spoke. I could hardly imagine what that old woman thought when she got the message from her neighbor that her daughter-in-law, her son, and their children were on a flight to the United States.

Other parents understood and gave their children their blessing. Dan Ha's husband, Binh, felt he couldn't leave the country without telling his parents. Their response to him was one of encouragement: "We lived under the Communist rule in the North, and we cannot bear their inhumane treatment of people. It would be a blessing if any of our family members could leave and go live in another country."

Tuan, like many Vietnamese men I knew, would never leave without his parents' approval, and since he had failed to get it, I wasn't going to argue. Besides, I myself couldn't say I wholly disagreed with Tuan's parents. I had shared their feelings about seeing Saigon fall before.

"At least let me buy you dinner tonight," I told Tuan. I had forgotten to exchange my money, and I had 2 million piasters left. I carried them around, still banded in paper, in a Samsonite briefcase. The piasters wouldn't be good anywhere else, and at the rate the piaster was devaluing, they might not be worth much in Saigon for very long.

Tuan and I went to the best French restaurant in Saigon. La Cave catered to diplomats and executives, so I wondered what would become of it when the Communists came to town. Tuan and I had just ducked our heads in before the April storm that had been building all afternoon finally broke. Rain came down in straight, thick ropes. The menu was entirely in French, but that posed no problem: I knew exactly what I wanted for my last meal in Saigon. We ordered Scotch, some beer, and a red Bordeaux—why not? We had caviar and the finest chateaubriand. We were not the only ones at La Cave that night; almost all the tables were full. The main dining room had been taken over by the French chamber of commerce for the evening. They looked like they were celebrating something. At first I thought it was strange, and then I realized that for them, the overthrow of the Americans wasn't such a bad thing. The French had been here first, and they were not the ones fleeing.

Tuan and I enjoyed every decadent mouthful. When the bill arrived, it was just shy of 20,000 piasters. I reached for my Samsonite briefcase and opened it for our waiter. His eyes nearly popped out of his head when he saw the 2 million piasters floating around. I told him just to take whatever he wanted.

Four days after my departure, Tuan would go to the Cercle Sportif to clear out his locker, but he would arrive too late. The club had been looted, the lockers broken into, and Tuan's tennis stuff taken. He would not have any opportunities to play anyway. He was walking out empty-handed when a column of Communist tanks rolled by. A North Vietnamese soldier in baggy green trousers and a pith hat yelled down to Tuan to ask if he knew where the presidential palace was.

"Sure, I do," Tuan told him. "You are just on the other side of it." Rather than have Tuan explain how to navigate to the palace's front entrance, the soldier motioned for him to hop on the lead tank and accompany them. Tuan was not in his Saigon police uniform. As he told it to me many years later, Tuan rode up front on the tank with the North Vietnamese Army, all the way to the gates at the front entrance of the palace. Then, the same soldier who had asked Tuan for directions told him gruffly to get to the back of the tank. "We're going to ram this gate," he said, and they did.

Despite his help with storming the palace, the North Vietnamese still sentenced Tuan to reeducation camp. He stayed there three years doing manual labor as penance for being on the South Vietnamese police force. It was backbreaking work, every single day without respite.

During Tuan's time in the camp, his wife decided to try to make a run for it. Life was just too hard for her and their child in Saigon. They simply couldn't survive without Tuan's policeman salary. Food was hard to come by, their home was taken by the state "for the people," and there was little hope that conditions would improve when Tuan got out of reeducation camp. The whole family would be branded as elements of the former regime, and it was unclear if her son could ever move past such a stigma in this new society. If she could only make it out of Vietnam, and come somehow to the United States, she thought she could get in touch with me. Together, we would eventually send for Tuan. So she bought two spots on a fishing boat. Between 1975 and 1985, one estimate I have heard puts the number of fleeing Vietnamese at 1.5 million. But they didn't all make it. There were storms at sea, and worse: Thai pirates and nightmare stories of women who were raped and of children who cried too loud and were tossed overboard. Tuan's wife and their four-year-old child never made it to the United States. Their overcrowded fishing boat capsized in the South China Sea, and everyone on board drowned.

After reeducation camp, Tuan moved back to Saigon. He eventually remarried, and he and his wife have four wonderful children.

In their home, a modest three-room apartment in Saigon, a black-and-white eight-by-ten photograph shows Tuan's first wife and child smiling down from their position above a family altar. Joss sticks are lit, and fresh fruit is put out for their spirits, but seeing it, I can't help wonder what would have happened if Tuan's parents had just said yes, and they had left with me.

CHAPTER 16

April 26, Flying Out

W hen I left my villa in Saigon for the last time, it was hours before dawn on Saturday, April 26, 1975. Everything was dark.
I don't remember the stars that night, or any winking lights of aircraft. Everything not blacked out by the nighttime curfew was obscured by rainclouds. I still had no idea how many divisions of the
North Vietnamese Army were close to the city. They were no longer
bothering to hide.

Breakfast was ready for me before I came downstairs. My housekeeper, Tao, was a good cook, and I knew I would miss her. So I took
my time, enjoying every bite and a cup of tea. It seemed it was the
first time all week that I was not rushing. I hugged my housekeeper
good-bye and thanked her for all her help. Then I gave her the rest
of the quickly depreciating South Vietnamese piasters and told her
to spend them as quickly as possible. "Anything else you want in
the house is yours," I told her. There was a tuxedo still hanging in
the closet and golf clubs in the shed. It was an inside joke with myself, imagining the face of a North Vietnamese general when con-
fronted with these imperialist artifacts, the remnants of my capitalist
life. The one thing I did take with me was my London Fog raincoat,
lightweight but long.

I drove myself back to the airport one last time, going carefully and slowly so it wouldn't look as if I were running away. The rain hadn't started up again yet, so the windows were down, a detail I thought helped me look casual. The main roads were lined with sandbags and concertina wire. I could hear the South Vietnamese Army soldiers talking behind the emplacements and see the tips of their glowing cigarettes. I was very aware that I was breaking a curfew that was supposed to last until dawn. I fully expected to be stopped and checked at any moment. I can't imagine what I would have said.

When I finally arrived at the airport parking lot, the field was already littered with other abandoned vehicles—Peugeots, Mercedes-Benzes, and Fords. I parked the blue rally wagon and pocketed the keys after locking it. I was picking my way through the metal carcasses toward the terminal when I thought better of it. The van had served us well, especially these last few days ferrying the staff to the airport. Whoever gets this van will get a good vehicle, I thought. So I went back, unlocked the driver's door, and put the key in the ignition.

I never did hear the famous signal for the evacuation of Saigon. The public affairs officer at the DAO had worked it out weeks earlier, but that officer was killed on the orphans' flight that crashed, Operation Babylift. Chuck Neil, the Armed Forces Radio announcer, was supposed to read the words, "The temperature in Saigon is 105 degrees and rising." This was to be followed by a recording of "I'm Dreaming of a White Christmas" played continuously. Some say the announcer finally got the call to put in the track after the bombing of Tan Son Nhut on Monday, but I don't know that anyone actually heard the recording. In any case, by the time the DAO signaled for the real evacuation to begin, it was too late for just about anyone who wasn't already inside the embassy gates.[1]

The last FNCB group of employees and husbands of employees was waiting for me at the tennis courts. They had spent all of Friday night there. I felt a bit bad about the nice shave and shower I had had in my villa. Because of my white skin, I lived like a little prince all over Asia. In some places, we were called "white devils," and the locals made fun of our big noses and hairy legs, but in practice, whites were deferred to and given preferential treatment. The racial lines were especially vivid in anything having to do with the evacuation. As long as I was by myself, no one bothered me at all, whether it was in the van or walking into the evacuation center without having to show any documentation. There were military checkpoints all along the road to Tan Son Nhut, but they dropped their barbed wire when I had come along alone that morning. Nobody stopped me unless I was with a Vietnamese person. Then it was an interrogation. I would come to learn that the final evacuation by helicopter was marked by the same blatant racism. Asians, even with a US passport, were turned away at the embassy gates while any white face, American or not, was pulled inside.[2]

Chi's husband, Van, the lieutenant colonel in the South Vietnamese Air Force, sat right next to me on the bus taking us from the tennis courts out to where the C-130 waited for us, engine already thrumming to leave. The rear loading ramp was down. It reminded me of Moby Dick, an open-mouthed whale ready to swallow us whole. That wasn't what made Van grab my arm in fright.

"I can't—I can't get out," he stammered. "John, I cannot go with you on this flight."

"You've got to, Van," I told him.

He shook his head. "That's my general, standing right by the gate. If he sees me, he might shoot me, right here."

I squinted into the drizzle. A half dozen men were milling around by the ramp, and I saw an older, portly man in a blue Vietnamese Air Force uniform with all the military markings of a general—I assumed he was the general Van was afraid of. But we couldn't turn around now. We were so close. I snatched up my long raincoat lying on the seat between us. "You are coming with us, Van. You'll get under my raincoat, and I'll hide you." *Or else I'll die trying*, I thought, but left that last bit unsaid.

The rain picked up. Thick drops streaked down the windows of the bus. I had the coat up over my head as if I were shielding myself from the weather. When I stepped off the bus, Van dove under the coat with me. He was squeezed against my left side, hiding underneath the coat's overhang. It was hot as hell, but I could feel his body shivering with fear next to me. As it would turn out, the air force general Van was so afraid would shoot him for desertion was getting out of Saigon too. He was on the very next flight out.

There were few seats in that roaring cavern, and it was too tight to sit down anyway, so I stood all the way to Guam. Thick nylon cargo straps ran across the floor, but it was hard to see what else was around me, with so many people standing and squatting on metal flooring. Very quickly, the ramp was closed, and the pilot taxied to the runway, turned sharply, and took off.

The appropriately named Hercules had four powerful engines. We used the same kind of plane a lot when I was in the service with SOG. We had painted ours black, but this one was army green. Otherwise the plane was just as I remembered. The steep angle of the climb made everyone slide back. Inside we were fighting for balance while the pilot was trying to navigate to keep the plane over friendly territory, a rapidly shrinking zone. Saigon retreated below us, and then we were above the surface-to-air missile range and over the Rung Sat, the "swamp of death" that lies between Saigon and the sea. My last glimpse of Vietnam was of green, and then it was lost in the dull grey clouds.

I was not the only representative of an American company who came back for Vietnamese employees. I heard that CBS news executives flew over from New York to see what they could do for the many Vietnamese who had helped them through the years. I never did find out what happened to the staff of the other American banks in Saigon. Bank of America and Chase were much larger than we were, so on the optimistic end, they may have had more support getting out. On the other hand, if the staffs were too big, it may have proved unwieldy to evacuate so many. I certainly had my hands full with just our staff members and their immediate families. Had our branch been bigger, would I still have been able to get them all out of Saigon?

Thi Dau, one of the FNCB Saigon employees, had a brother-in-law who worked for Bank of America. He left on a bus like the one a few of the FNCB spouses took, coordinated by the US embassy for American commercial interests in Saigon. But he must have left on a bus that departed after ours, because he had a harrowing story. By the time his bus got to the DAO, the gate was locked. Vietnamese soldiers wouldn't open up. According to his memory of what happened, tanks came out of the DAO and surrounded the American-led buses, forcing them to retreat. Thi Dau's brother-in-law and sister ended up leaving on a navy boat that was part of the US Seventh Fleet. (They were surprised to see the former South Vietnamese premier, Nguyen Cao Ky, on deck with them.) Thi Dau's brother-in-law was eventually relocated to San Francisco, where he got a new job within Bank of America.

IBM had set up a situation room in Guam to coordinate the evacuation of their 154 South Vietnamese employees, but their story was frustratingly similar to what we had gone through in Hong Kong, trying to arrange planes and airlifts. The difference was that they were still in planning mode, and I had gone into Saigon. One of

IBM's senior Vietnamese staff was in daily contact with Ashida, the economic attaché. As he had done with Chuyen on our staff, Ashida made promises to IBM but stalled on delivery.[3] He stalled too long.

On April 28, two days after I left Saigon, fourteen North Vietnamese Army divisions surrounded the city. They were armed with antiaircraft weapons but never used them on an evacuating flight. The airport was bombed at dusk on the twenty-eighth to signal their imminent arrival. The heavy bombing started the next morning. It rendered the runways useless and put an end to all fixed-wing traffic, which meant no more evacuations by airplane. Anyone leaving after that had to get out of the city by helicopter or boat. The embassy had made a plan for such an event; it even had a name, Operation Frequent Wind. But nothing proceeded on schedule. There were more refugees than the embassy expected. There was confusion and bad weather. There were not enough helicopters to get everyone out, but even if there had been, there were not enough ships offshore for the helicopters to land. American crews resorted to pitching helicopters off the side of the ships and into the sea to make room for more choppers to land.

In the eighteen hours before Saigon finally fell to the Communists, seventy helicopters and 865 marines made 630 flights out. They took 1,373 Americans and 5,595 Vietnamese, plus nearly 1,000 from other countries. They would join the nearly 40,000 refugees who had already been evacuated from Saigon between April 1 and April 29.[4] But it wasn't nearly enough. Tens of thousands of Vietnamese were left behind. A huge crowd mobbed the outside walls of the embassy compound. Desperate Vietnamese tried to claw their way up the ten-foot wall, only to be knocked back by rifle butts and marines in battle gear. Some tried to jump the wall and landed on barbed wire strung along the top. People held up their children, begging the departing Americans to take them with them.

The chief strategy analyst for the CIA, Frank Snepp, was ashamed:

> When my time came to leave that night, with the last CIA contingent in the Embassy, we had to push Vietnamese out of the way in the halls to get to the chopper on the roof. I couldn't look into their eyes.
>
> Retreat is the most difficult of all military operations. But as a matter of honor you do not leave friends on the battlefield. In the evacuation of Saigon over half of the Vietnamese who finally got out escaped on their own with no help from us until they were far at sea.

It was five o'clock in the morning on April 30 when the American ambassador, Graham Martin, got on a CH-46 helicopter. He was one of the last civilians to leave before President Ford ordered an end to the airlift. Three hours later, the last Americans to be flown out of South Vietnam were eleven marines who had guarded the end of the evacuation, throwing gas grenades behind them to stop the terrified Vietnamese from charging the last helicopter. At eleven thirty a.m. on April 30, 1975, the revolutionary flag went up over Saigon's presidential palace. The Communists had won.[5]

CHAPTER 17

The End of April

—————————————————

BEFORE EVERYONE LEFT SAIGON, I had given the leader of each small group an FNCB datebook. We had stacks lying around the bank; they were one of our giveaways to customers and clients. The datebook was navy blue, with the gold seal of the bank embossed on the front. Printed on the first pages were the address and phone number of every FNCB branch in Asia, from Brunei to Mauritius to Hong Kong. I had no idea where the planes were taking the 106 people, but I told them that when they landed, they should contact the nearest bank office. They should tell them that they were from FNCB Saigon. I wasn't sure what would happen after that.

—————————————————

I took my own advice. One of the first things I did as soon as I landed was find a phone. That wasn't as easy as it sounds. The airport in Guam was not like any airport I had ever seen before. It was a field of tents surrounded by a barbed-wire fence. MPs guarded both sides. I was an American, so I was allowed to roam freely. The guards were there to keep the Vietnamese contained.

I finally got through to Rick Roesch, senior vice president of the bank and the head of the Asia Pacific Division.

"Rick, it's John Riordan. Everyone is out of Saigon. I'm in Guam, and I think most of our staff is here too. I . . . well, I just felt that someone at the bank should know."

"John! We're just popping champagne bottles here, John, to celebrate! Congratulations! You're a hero. You've done a great job."

I was dazed. It had been a terribly long week. Was I dreaming this? I could barely believe what I was hearing. "Great job"? Did that mean that I still had a job?

Within a day, the answer came by telex. It was sent to Guam's FNCB branch, addressed to me from Head Office.

JOHN IT IS TRULY IMPOSSIBLE TO CONVEY BY TELEX THE ADMIRATION AND WARMTH YOUR ACTIONS IN SAI-GON HAVE GENERATED HERE IN NEW YORK STOP GET SOME REST ASAP LOOK FORWARD TO SEEING YOU VERY SOON

It was signed "Crouse/Howell"—the two vice presidents from New York who had called me at the beginning of April to tell me to close the bank and get out of Saigon.

Unbeknownst to me, Head Office in New York City had jumped into action the moment the first FNCB staff arrived from Saigon and called one of the bank numbers from the datebook. The local branches in Guam and Clark Air Force Base were mobilized to help. Bob Wilcox, the general manager of the Guam branch, and his wife arrived at Camp Asan with boxes of clothes and supplies—everything from toothbrushes to baby formula. Mike McTighe must have finally gotten his passport back, because he flew down from Hong Kong.

I explained the story over and over again. I had adopted the Vietnamese to get them out of South Vietnam. For many of my adoptees, it was the first time they heard of it. They were all my children now.

I gave them a lot of credit for taking it so well. Everyone seemed to understand it was a desperate measure. Instead of being angry with me, they just laughed and made a joke of it. The staff told me I was going to be in a whole lot of trouble when it came time to make up my will.

The adoption play had gotten the FNCB staff out of Saigon, but it wasn't going to be enough to get 106 people into the United States. A letter on FNCB letterhead was immediately delivered to the admiral in command of refugee processing in Guam.

> *You may consider this letter a firm, irrevocable commitment of*
> *First National City Bank to guarantee the financial capacity of*
> *all Vietnamese bank employees and their dependents presently*
> *under the custody of the Department of Defense in various*
> *Guam refugee centers.*

Head Office in New York had already reached out to Bob Hudspeth. He was the branch manager in Saigon who had preceded McTighe, and in fact, he had set up the whole office. He had left FNCB for a job with another bank but was taking time away from his job to fly in from Singapore to help the FNCB team at the headquarters on Park Avenue match the Saigon personnel to any available positions in FNCB's branches.

When Hudspeth arrived in the conference room in New York's Head Office, the walls were already covered with pieces of paper— one for each employee. Every conceivable detail was scrawled in black ink: what languages they spoke, when they had been hired, what their responsibilities had been in Saigon. They asked Bob to help them think through which branches with available positions might be the best match. For example, people with Chinese backgrounds went to branches near Chinatown. The three single women on the staff were sent to branches in central San Francisco, out of consideration that they had not learned how to drive and San Francisco had great public transportation. Hudspeth and the rest of the personnel department made every effort to match the person to the job. They also sent word to the branches that would be receiving the Vietnamese staff of FNCB. Branches around the country devoted staff time and resources to preparing orientation materials. The staff would be given basic information on how to live in the United States, and someone was assigned to help them with their first shopping trips and their first commutes to work.

Chi's husband, Van, whom I had hidden under my raincoat at the airport, was not on the FNCB staff before the evacuation. But now that his country no longer existed, he needed to find a new line of work. FNCB hired Van as a security guard at the branch near Kennedy Airport and he took an Americanized name for his new life in his new country. He took my name, John.

The bank sponsored clothing and furniture drives to get the South Vietnamese settled into their new communities. Some people were hosted in their new cities by FNCB employees who were themselves refugees of Communism. For example, the Phams stayed with the Zarudas in Chicago. The Zarudas had survived Communism in Czechoslovakia, and they had volunteered right away to host a family coming in from South Vietnam. Mrs. Zaruda taught Mr. Pham how to operate small household electrical appliances and how to find coupons, and she went shopping with him at the grocery store, while Mr. Zaruda and Thi Coi (Mrs. Pham) left at six a.m. every day for work in downtown Chicago.

FNCB loaned every employee half a year's salary with no interest. That made it possible for many of the staff to get on their feet. The bank also reimbursed tuition for any college or continuing education classes. There was never squabbling over which profit center was going to pick up the costs. Everyone at the bank was in this one together. The FNCB staff who were relocated to the New York City area were put up by the bank at the San Carlos Hotel on Fiftieth Street and Third Avenue for one month. Each family was given money for shopping: $500 per staff member, $300 for each dependent. Buses with tour guides were rented to show the Vietnamese around the city; FNCB human resources personnel came to take the families to parks and organized picnics. The figure I heard bandied about was that it cost the bank $1 million to resettle the Vietnamese, but it seems to me that it had to have been much more than that.

For all the effort the bank put in, it was still hard on the Saigon staff adjusting to a new country. Communication was constantly a hurdle. Although everyone at the bank read and wrote English, they weren't used to speaking it and hearing it around them all the time. There were words the staff had never used before, and they had to navigate totally foreign contexts like dryers at the Laundromat and strange-looking fruits and vegetables at the grocery store. One of our accounting staff, Ha, told me how humbling it was. Because of her poor language skills, the only job the bank had been able to place her in was a typing job, reporting to another typist. She was the secretary's secretary. "I felt deaf and dumb," Ha confided to me.

Homesickness for many of the Vietnamese was crippling. Ha put words to the feelings so many of our staff had: "I felt like I had been sent to the moon, and would never have a chance to return back home." The children marveled at pizza delivery and ubiquitous candy vending machines, but for the adults, it was years before some of them dared to try a McDonald's hamburger. Some families living in Los Angeles were too intimidated to step foot in Disneyland. They felt they didn't belong in the United States, and it was no wonder.

From what I read in the newspaper, there seemed to be a strong, growing anti-refugee feeling, especially in California, where so many Vietnamese ended up. The influx of Southeast Asian refugees had created pressure on an already tight job market. Unemployment was at a record high that year, and there were demonstrations in the streets.

Minh, Dung's new husband, felt uneasy being in the United States. He had studied in New Zealand and wasn't sure that coming to America was the best fit for them. As he said to me, "I was not sure what treatment we would get from the public when we got out of the camp. I discussed with Dung about leaving the USA to go settle in New Zealand, where we would not be unwelcome. Dung said that she would go with me to wherever I went." They went from Camp Pendleton to Auckland the week after they arrived.

But all that was still to come. Before anyone could move on to the next step, there was the misery of the refugee camps while their status was being processed. For people who were accustomed to professional, urban, modern lives, it was a painful adjustment. Everything required waiting in line. They waited in line to complete paperwork. They waited in line for the showers or the bathroom. There were more lines for anything to eat or drink, and sometimes the lines were so long that they had to line up again as soon as they finished eating.

There wasn't enough room for the flood of refugees in one camp, so more camps had to be built, more tents erected. Bulldozers smoothed the earth, but all the construction made dust go everywhere. Large, olive-drab tents were pitched; cots were being off-loaded from trucks; medical and other supplies were streaming in. Guam is the southernmost island in the Mariana chain, just east of the Philippines. The island is only thirty miles long and four to twelve miles wide. It was a little late for typhoon season, but at the end of April there was a major one heading straight toward the island. Meteorologists were predicting winds over one hundred miles an hour. If it hit, no one could imagine what the island would do with the one hundred thousand refugees living in tents. There was nowhere for them to go. The island's population had already practically doubled over the last week. Thankfully the typhoon veered off course and headed northeast, but it was a close one.

Bob Wilcox, the general manager of the Guam branch of FNCB, couldn't stand to see the Saigon employees herded like cattle around the refugee camps. The conditions got squalid quickly. One of his bank's clients was a hotel by the sea. He arranged to have FNCB rent the entire place. Each bungalow had two bedrooms, one bathroom, a kitchenette, and a small table. Except for the biggest families, the staff tried to squeeze two families into each one. The bank privately coordinated food, and got infant formula and baby food for the youngest children. The kids' resilience was immediately on display. They ran up and down the beach, kicking balls and playing tag and hide and seek. One of the evacuees, just eight years old at the time, recalls eating fresh tomatoes picked off the vine and playing "all day as if there was no tomorrow and no yesterday." But the older children, those who knew what was happening, struggled. Kien's son wrote:

> For me, the most intense feeling I had at the time was guilt. I did not understand why we are so lucky, why we got out while all [the other] people we knew would live in fears and face unknown future, guilty for leaving my homeland during the most darkness time. Did we just waste twenty years from 54 to 75? Did we waste million of

lives on both sides for nothing? At the same time I felt relieved, free, no longer living in fears, afraid of retribution from Viet Cong. All of us knew we were so lucky, so grateful to get out when we did with the whole family intact. So many other families were not so fortunate; they were split up; some got to freedom, some stayed behind, endured years of suffer[ing].

Many of the South Vietnamese staff had not had time to say good-bye to their families. That separation, from family and country, was dislocating and painful.

On April 30, 1975, the FNCB staff from Saigon was gathered on the beach for a barbecue picnic hosted by FNCB Guam. Huy put on his radio to listen to music, but the party was interrupted by a news broadcast out of Vietnam. The president of the Republic of South Vietnam, Duong Van Minh, who had only been in place forty-eight hours, announced his unconditional surrender. At 10:24 a.m., just hours after the final evacuation, Minh went on the radio to announce:

> The Republic of Vietnam policy is the policy of peace and reconciliation, aimed at saving the blood of our people. We are here waiting for the Provisional Revolutionary Government to hand over the authority in order to stop useless bloodshed.

President Minh had waited for the Communists on the top steps of the presidential palace. He and thirty of his advisors had set up two rows of chairs to greet their victors. When the first Communist tank crashed through the palace gates at 11:10 a.m., Minh said, "The revolution is here. You are here." Minh went on the radio again that afternoon to announce to the people: "I declare the Saigon government is completely dissolved at all levels."

Someone on the staff of FNCB began to sing "Vietnam, Vietnam." Before that day, I had heard the song sung in national celebrations, always against tinny background music with a lot of strings. It had sounded to my untrained ear something like a polka. It was nothing like the a cappella version, accompanied by waves lapping on the beach and tears. One voice joined with another in a powerful, moving expression of irretrievable loss.

Unlike the other South Vietnamese ex-presidents, like Thieu and Nguyen Cao Ky, Minh did not flee. He was arrested after his official surrender, but he was treated leniently by the Communist government. Minh lived in an unofficial home arrest, secluded in his villa for eight years, continuing to grow exotic orchids and raise birds. In 1983, Minh was allowed to immigrate to France. He lived near Paris until he finally moved to Pasadena. He passed away in 2001.

Much to my surprise, McTighe was already in Guam and waiting for me when I landed. I never did sort out how he found out where I was going, much less how he knew what flight I'd be on. But McTighe must have gotten his passport back, because there he was. Despite my exhaustion, I smiled at him in open amazement. I had done it.

"Great to see you here, John. You've done a terrific job." McTighe shook my hand sincerely. But with the congratulatory remarks dispensed with, the smile vanished from his face. McTighe immediately got serious. "As it turns out," McTighe said, "I have one more job for you."

"I need you to get on a plane and go to Clark Air Force Base," he said as he looked at me from beneath his bushy blonde eyebrows knitted together with concern.

All I wanted was rest. I thought I deserved a good night's sleep.

"Now?" I spluttered incredulously.

McTighe nodded seriously. "John, Mr. Huy's wife has just had her baby. You need to get down there. You need to see if she needs anything." McTighe delivered his order and nodded, as if it were already done. I should have asked him why he didn't go himself. He obviously had his passport back. Maybe I was too tired to protest, or maybe I really did just want to see if she were okay. So I went.

Huy's wife, Van, had been part of the first group that left Saigon. She had gone into labor a few hours after she landed at the refugee camp. The baby was early; stress and anxiety probably played a big role in his premature birth. But the baby was strong and healthy, as was his mother. Huy and his wife named the baby Phillip Clark, after the Philippines and Clark Air Force Base.

Looking back on these events nearly forty years later, I can tell you that I am honored to have these people in my life and to have been made so much a part of theirs. They still call me Papa, or Father, names I have not heard anywhere else in my life. The crying and frightened children huddling together in the airport in 1975 have since grown up. Some of them have graduated from Ivy League universities. They are lawyers and doctors, homemakers and beauty technicians, and, of course, bankers.

Many have had their own children, so I suppose I'm some kind of grandfather now. I started with 32 of FNCB's employees and adopted them, along with their immediate families, bringing the number to 106. By my latest count, they have multiplied through marriage and children and grandchildren to at least 254; we are unable to verify but estimate that it may be closer to 275 or more, and the group is still growing. That number does not include the extended family that most of my children successfully sponsored from Vietnam. With those relatives we would be at 1,000, or higher.

THE END OF APRIL

L ast April, I received an email that was simply written but heart-felt from the daughter of one of my adoptees. Her father had died. I was sorry; I remembered him as a kind and thoughtful man. But she wasn't writing for sympathy. Somehow she had found my email with his things, and she was simply thanking me for saving her life, thirty-nine years before:

> Around this time every year, we always ask ourselves what
> would happen to us if we were left behind in Viet Nam. How
> our father could survive the communist regime, knowing that
> he had once escaped North Viet Nam in 1954. It's unthinkable
> of what would have happen[ed] if we did not get out of Viet
> Nam! Again, my family and I are forever grateful to you.

I am genuinely touched by thanks like this, even if it makes me feel a bit awkward. I remind them as often as I can that there are other people to thank, but some are dead or have faded completely back into the shadows. Most of us who went through that harried escape together are spread out in different corners of the United States, from Connecticut to California. A few of us stay in touch by email and telephone, some get together socially, but many I haven't seen or talked to in years. There have been a few opportunities for a reunion, and I still have to be talked into going, but I have found it easier to accept than to protest too much. You can't imagine how moving it is to be hugged around the knees by a small child who looks up at you and says, "Thank you for rescuing my family, Papa John." I am humbled by the attention and affection. When I am greeted, there are bouquets of flowers at the airport, intense days of eating and drinking, meeting new husbands and congratulations on graduations, and, of course, reminiscing about what we made it through.

I live on a farm now, about an hour away from Milwaukee, Wisconsin. My life is ordered—I follow the pace the seasons set and take care to make good with my neighbors. I'm someone who tries to follow the rules of life and obey chains of command. I had to, however, bend some of my principles during the evacuation in order to save the lives of my Vietnamese coworkers and friends. Thinking back on my last weeks in Saigon, to that brief moment I stepped outside my usual ordered self, is like catching a familiar actor in an old movie you had never known they starred in. I disobeyed my bosses, defied the US government's directive to stay in Saigon, and perjured myself on official documents. I also set fire to more than $1 million. Amazingly, it all seems to have worked out okay—except for those few who couldn't, or wouldn't, come with me when I asked. And there were thousands of South Vietnamese I couldn't take, but who were American friends and allies, left behind.

I've returned to Vietnam three times since my hasty departure in 1975. The first time was in 2008. I went to Hanoi, curious to see the city that my friends had nightmares about. I had been somewhat worried about my arrival, thinking my name might be on a blacklist in customs and immigration, but I sailed right through. I found the capital charming if a bit dull. North Vietnamese were gracious hosts, well practiced at not dwelling on the past in front of American tourists. I was less nervous when I returned in 2011 and 2013 to what had been home in Saigon and has since been renamed Ho Chi Minh City.

At first glance, everything had changed. Gleaming glass and metal towers—emblems of a rising financial metropolis—towered over scrubbed streets. The massage parlors and bars I used to stroll

past have been replaced with shop fronts displaying brightly polished lacquerware, silks, and amber jewelry right next to tech repair
shops to fix broken iPhones. Citibank opened a large branch a few
blocks away from the property we rented in 1975; signs advertise
its banking services all over town, and the website tells me there
are now twenty-five Citibank ATM kiosks within city limits spitting
out Vietnamese currency at 21,000 dong to the dollar. I eventually
found my bearings while walking from the Central Market to the
cathedral, in between the traffic circles and tree-lined boulevards,
catching glimpses of the old city I had loved.

The Hotel Continental has been rebuilt: the open-air terrace has
been all glassed in. The hotel was and still is a Vietnamese institution. I went there a great deal in my military and banking days in
Saigon; it was an unforgettable part of my Vietnam experience. Over
the years the Hotel Continental has hosted many famous poets and
writers, including Graham Greene, author of the novel *The Quiet
American*, in which the hotel features prominently.

The Cercle Sportif, the once-exclusive, members-only sports club
where I spent so many happy weekend afternoons in the pool or on
the tennis court, also still exists. Now you can buy admission by the
day for less than a dollar.

Except in the darkest shadow of Ho Chi Minh City's alleyways,
the grit is gone. In its place is a palatable sense of opportunity and
optimism.

The street I lived on has been renamed, as have most streets in
the city. It is called Dien Bien Phu, after the decisive battle in the
Communist-led victory over the French in 1954. It is still a major
thoroughfare through the city. A high fence and long drive always
made the villa seem private and protected it from much of the traffic
sounds and exhaust. In my day, I could hear the street, but faintly.
Then there was the splash of rubber bicycle tires, along with army

trucks clattering down the road. Now it's the sound of scooters and taxis blaring horns and revving engines to get somewhere quickly.

I suppose I knew that there had always been two villas at the end of the drive, but I had forgotten over time. It was hard at first to distinguish which one was mine: Building B. It looked bigger to me, and then I noticed an expansion for a large commercial kitchen. The villa's familiar white facade had been repainted a soft yellow, and the house had been turned into a cafe, serving light snacks and sweet syrupy drinks to well-heeled young Vietnamese who liked the clean lines of mid-century decor—retro chic. But I knew I was in the right place as soon as I saw those red-and-white floor tiles in the entry, bringing a bit of Moroccan style to the tropics of Southeast Asia.

My furniture, or rather, the furnishings the bank had provided me with, was long gone. Clusters of blond wood tables and low-slung sofas now overlooked a lush garden. The garden looked bigger to me too, and it was the one change I was sorry to see. The gnarled old banyan tree by the side of the garden had been taken down. Its broad canopy had provided me shady afternoons, relief from the tropical sun, shielding me and the house from the hottest part of the day. I had been partial to that tree. It was covered in a strange moss that gave the house the faraway feel of a Kipling book. But not everyone liked that tree. Visitors to my house had tried to warn me that banyans were always haunted.

It wasn't just my Vietnamese friends who had called the gnarled old thing a "ghost tree." Father Crawford, an Irish priest friend of mine in Saigon, had confided a story over drinks one night about an old woman who could sense phantoms because of her tree. I listened carefully because I had ghost stories in my own family. My grandmother saw the ghosts of her son and her murdered father. When I had written to my family from Vietnam, I added in the detail about my haunted villa in Saigon. Maybe it made my overseas posting with the bank seem even more exotic somehow, but I had trouble with flickering lights the whole time I lived in that house. I would have blamed it on Saigon's overwhelmed electric grid, but when the repair man came, he said he couldn't find any earthly reason for it.

To the Vietnamese, ghosts aren't bad, just tragically trapped spirits that can't escape. The city I called Saigon should be filled with them, the hundreds of thousands of people who tried so desperately to get out in the last days of Saigon but were left behind. There is a famous image of that desperation, taken by Hugh Van Es: a tenuous string to the frenzied mob below, most of them left behind, unable to climb aboard the last of the departing CIA helicopters. For Americans, that image has come to symbolize the entire colossal failure of the American effort in Vietnam. But what about the thousands of doomed Vietnamese who didn't make it on that flight or any others? According to the official line in Vietnam, people like that don't exist. The Communist Party has been successful in blotting out the less glorious events during the fall of Saigon and have supplanted it with propaganda. The state-approved image is one of successful tanks busting through the palace gates and of people gratefully welcoming their liberators. The ghosts of thousands who died after the Communist victory are silenced.

In the years since 1975, I've come to appreciate more about the man we called our enemy for so many years, Ho Chi Minh. He did say that the Communists would rebuild Vietnam "ten times more beautiful," and eventually, his words came to pass. But the intervening years were awful. As many as four hundred thousand Southerners who fought or worked for Americans or the ousted South Vietnam regime were rounded up and forced into reeducation camps. These were not just soldiers but doctors, bankers, lawyers, engineers, and artists. The same people who could have helped rebuild the country after devastating decades of war were forced to perform menial labor and waste time writing "self-criticisms." Then there were those who drowned or were killed by pirates when they tried to flee by boat, or fell sick from malnutrition and disease that plagued the country during eleven miserable years of rice shortages wrought by a centrally planned economic tailspin. The victors would prefer to have us believe that everyone was successfully re-educated and absorbed into the expanding and thriving economy. But if the Communists have an amazing capacity for delusion, so do the Americans. Our country tried for decades to forget the shameful act of abandoning our allies. Veterans of Vietnam were outcasts, and our eyes were averted from the failure in Southeast Asia and replaced with American grandiosity.

My actions in Saigon in April 1975 were motivated by one simple belief: it was the right thing to do. People often get that wrong; mistakes get made for the right reasons all the time. Maybe I got lucky. I could have played it safe. I could have stayed away. In fact, in the context of the times, staying away would have been understandable, even advisable. I wasn't trying to be a hero, but it seemed right to me to at least try to help my colleagues and my friends. When I could not stand by, they all became my family. Now they have become our neighbors, our friends, and our fellow Americans. In the case of these 106 lives, the tragic and chaotic end of the Vietnam War became the beginning of something new.

Epilogue

WATCHING THE AMERICAN involvement in Iraq and Afghanistan wind down is like watching a replay of the past. We should have learned our lesson then: when you get into wars, you need to figure out how to get out of them. It is hard for me to escape the cold memory of seeing so many Vietnamese left behind during the fall of Saigon. I did my part, but the United States left behind tens, maybe hundreds, of thousands of South Vietnamese, just when they needed our help the most. Today, the most vulnerable Iraqis and Afghans are those who worked alongside Americans. The US government has not made any plans public about how it intends to protect them. Bureaucratic procedures to procure exit visas are messy; thousands remain in procedural limbo, waiting for a visa. The official American stance on this looming crisis seems to shadow the stubborn optimism of the American ambassador in Saigon back in 1975, Graham Martin. Washington and the State Department are trying to convince themselves that Iraq and Afghanistan are in better shape than they are. The truth of it is that unless a plan is developed, we are leaving them behind, just as so many were left behind in Vietnam.

The upside of the Vietnamese refugee crisis was that it resulted in the creation of a dynamic Vietnamese American community. All the Vietnamese Americans I have known celebrate the fact that they have moved far beyond their refugee origins to become successful economic and political players in US society.

In 1975, President Gerald Ford signed the Indochina Migration and Refugee Act. It granted refugees from Vietnam, Cambodia, and Laos special status to enter the United States. The bill was amended a few years later to permit refugees to adjust to a parolee status and later become permanent residents. By then, the first wave of refugees, the people who escaped South Vietnam before the fall, had been relatively settled. A second major exodus out of Vietnam began in 1978 and lasted into the mid-1980s. The total was almost two million people.[1] Secretary of State Cyrus Vance told Congress in July 1979:

> We are a nation of refugees. Most of us can trace our presence here to the turmoil or oppression of another time and another place. Our nation has been immeasurably enriched by this continuing process. We will not turn our backs on our traditions. We must meet the commitments we have made to other nations and to those who are suffering. In doing so, we will also be renewing our commitments to our ideals.[2]

The Vietnamese I helped bring to the United States live a diversity of normal American lives, which is, in itself, extraordinary. Thi Dau, one of the FNCB staff I helped evacuate, summed it up this way: "I have a busy schedule. I practice Tai Chi on Mondays and Fridays. Tuesday, I do yoga. Wednesday, therapeutic exercise and computer. Thursday, zumba, Friday, meditation. Every morning, when I go to the gym, I feel very happy. I can exercise and have fun with my friends instead of working in the rice fields under the hot sun, or get locked up in the communist jail."

I took a poll recently to see how big the families of the original evacuees have gotten. We've more than doubled in size. The original group of 106 has grown to at least 254; we are unable to verify but estimate that it may be closer to 275 or more. There has also been an exponential result from bringing the FNCB staff to the United States. When they became citizens, a process that took roughly five years from what I heard, they in turn sponsored more Vietnamese to immigrate to the United States. For instance, Ha's family sponsored over twenty relatives and friends, and Hoa sponsored thirteen, including her parents, brothers, and sisters. After she got her MBA, Xuan sponsored her parents and her extended family. All of them shared their homes and their food until the people they helped bring over found jobs of their own and were able to pay rent.

Many of the people I helped get out of Saigon have found their way back to Vietnam, either professionally or as tourists. Tran Minh Ha, who had to start her career over in the United States as a secretary's secretary because of her difficulty in English, stayed with Citibank for thirty years. She rose through the ranks, becoming a vice president of the global trade division. She was part of a trade advisory team that worked with Citibank branches all over the world. It was her work that finally took her back to Vietnam, but never to stay longer than a week. Still, she went two or three times a year over a period of ten years to conduct international trade seminars.

My secretary, Betty, went back in 1996 to visit her family. Until 1984, every time she sent a letter home, she would receive back only a form letter stating that the letter had been received. After a while, Betty learned that she could send packages. She packed them with sugar, flour, cooking oil, and material for clothes. Betty's mother scratched out a living in Saigon by reselling the things her daughter sent to her. The family that had once had maids to cook and clean was living in poverty. When Betty went back to reunite with her family, what she found took her breath away. "The Communists forced my family to burn every picture of me and everything with my name on it. [Even] my recipe book was destroyed." Betty couldn't help but wonder what they would have done to her if they had found her instead of her things.

When Cuc went back to Vietnam in 2009, she moved there with her husband and her oldest son. That son, who had been two and a half years old during the evacuation of 1975, had been the victim of a terrible car accident as a teenager. It paralyzed him and left him with a severe brain injury. Cuc and her husband, Kinh, thought that medical care and in-home help might be more affordable in Vietnam than in the United States. It didn't work out—the care wasn't what Cuc had hoped for her son. It might have been more affordable, but the rest of life was too difficult. They returned home to the United States and to their other two children, a neurologist daughter and a son in finance.

When Chuyen went back to Vietnam, it was in September 1993. He went to reopen a Citibank office. The bank had not had a presence in the country in nearly twenty years, and it still couldn't be fully operational, since the American trade embargo was still in place. There we igns that the embargo would be lifted soon, and Citibank wantea ω be ready. Who better to run the new branch than Chuyen? He said, "I switched off the lights," when we left in 1975, and he "never dreamed" he'd be switching them on again. After all, the embargo barred the World Bank and other development lenders from making loans to Vietnam.

When Chuyen returned, in many ways, he found the infrastructure the same as when he had left. Only 10 percent of the roads were paved, and much of the country was without a reliable source of electricity. The American trade embargo could partly be blamed for Vietnam's lag, but the problems ran deeper than that. Vietnam had no commercial code, no bankruptcy law, and no regulations to support a modern banking system. Vietnam was trying to bring the legal system up to date and into line with its aspirations, but the result was often chaotic.

Yet Chuyen was excited to be a part of the change. It was a challenging job, dealing with Hanoi and licensing, and Chuyen enjoyed it, but Vietnam, as long as it was run by the Communists, was no longer home for him. After successfully starting up two offices, one in Hanoi and one in Ho Chi Minh City, Chuyen returned home to the United States.[3]

When I finally got back to the United States in the summer of 1975, I checked in at the FNCB Head Office on Park Avenue. Things had worked out for the Vietnamese staff, and I hoped that things would work out for me. I hadn't been back long when I happened to be walking down one of the bank's corridors, and I ran into George Vojta. It had been Vojta who had told me that under no circumstances was I to go back to Vietnam. I'm sure it had been Vojta who had taken the shit that rained down when it was discovered I was gone. Obviously, now that the Vietnamese were safe, things had mellowed. I knew I wasn't in too much trouble with the bank, but I wondered how it might affect my career. And I was still tense about running into Vojta, whom I had so blatantly defied.

"John," Vojta said as he strode down the hall toward me. He had three or four senior officers tagging along behind him, struggling to keep up with their boss's purposeful stride. "Do you have a dime on you?" he asked.

"Ah, sure, yes I do, somewhere," I stammered. I was a little confused about why he would ask me for a dime when he was with people who could have found change for him. But I fumbled in my pocket.

When I produced the dime, Vojta snatched it out of my fingers. "That's your penalty, John. That was damned reckless of you to go back to Saigon," he admonished. A smile crinkled the corner of his eyes as he reached into the inside pocket of his suit jacket and pulled out an envelope to hand to me. "Here is your reward. Well done, John. Glad to have you back."

Inside the envelope was a check for five thousand dollars.

I traveled to other branches in Asia for FNCB until 1977, and then I returned to New York City. Chi, the head teller from Saigon and her husband, Van, whom I had smuggled to the plane under my raincoat, invited me to their home in Queens. They came to visit me when my parents were in town, cooking us a feast of Vietnamese food. Their six children adapted well to their new home, their new culture. It was Chi and Van's three boys who finally taught me how to throw and catch a football. And you know what? It was fun.

In 1985, I went to Cincinnati to testify in a trial, Ngoc Van Trinh versus Citibank. Trinh, the plaintiff, sought the return of 3 million piasters deposited by his father into a joint bank account at FNCB Saigon before the city fell. Trinh was a student in Michigan at the time, and he never returned to Vietnam. He became a US citizen in 1979, but his father was placed in a reeducation camp. In 1980, he sent the bank passbook to his son in Michigan, who tried to retrieve the deposit from Citibank's New York office. Citibank argued that the parent bank was not liable for that deposit, that instead the National Bank of Vietnam was, but the court ultimately ruled in the plaintiff's favor.

I took the stand to tell the story of those last weeks in Vietnam. It had very little to do with the case at hand, but the judge was so taken with the story that he made me keep going. He wanted to know what happened to the Vietnamese and if their lives had turned out well. He seemed pleased when I said that yes, for the most part, it did seem to work out well.

I resigned from the bank when I was forty years old, in 1982. I made some well-timed real estate investments in Manhattan and started making more off those than I ever had made at the bank. I finally moved out of the city altogether, to a farm in Wisconsin. I took a course in natural landscaping, and the property, a quarter mile square, keeps me busy. I burn prairie grass and tackle the weeds. I have to be vigilant to keep the white sweet clover down and the other invasive species out, but I've put aside plans for building a pond on the property. There's a delta area, where the creek spreads out, that used to be a Native American campground. About two hundred years ago, Native Americans portaged here, carrying their canoes overland from the Mississippi. They had to carry everything they possessed from one place to another. What they chose to bring with them, and what they left behind, reminds me of the brave voyage 106 Vietnamese made with me, forty years ago this April.

I've kept in touch with many of them, and I am grateful to them for their contributions to this book. Bank employees, spouses, and children sent in their own memories of what happened in those hectic last weeks in Saigon. The years have been long, and there are some things we remember a little differently. In those instances, I have done my best to cross-check dates, places, and people, and where that was impossible, I have relied on my own recollections of conversations and details.

All of the stories the Vietnamese submitted to me were filled with thanks and gratitude for my service to them. I am touched and humbled. I was doing what I felt I had to do, what I felt was the right thing to do. The most important thing was their safety, and I was glad to play a part. To their kind words below, I can only say thank you.

When I look back upon my life, I often wonder if the fortune teller I met as a 16 year old girl really had the ability to predict the future or was it all happenstance and coincidence. My present self would say neither. My present self would say that things happen because of the warm hearts of kind and caring people like Mr. John Riordan. He and the people at Citibank changed the fate of [106] of their employees and the generations to come. My husband and I are forever grateful for the opportunity that has been given to us and the smile on our children's and grandchildren's faces are a constant reminder of that generosity.

—BUI THI BICH LIEN

Now I have a very comfortable life. I could not have accomplished any of this without Mr. Riordan's taking a huge personal risk to get all of us out of Vietnam. The generosity of City Bank and the kindness of my co-workers and also the soldiers who helped us I will remember forever.

Mr. Riordan, City Bank, its staff and the kind U.S. military personnel are my angels who rescued me from what could have been a nightmare.

—NGUYEN NHUOC DAM

After 39 years, thinking of my unexpected and sudden journey to escape from the Communist regime, I feel so lucky to have joined FNCB (now called Citibank) and very thankful to the bank and its employees who helped us to evacuate from Vietnam and resettle in the US. Among the benefactors from Citibank, I am deeply grateful to Mr. John Riordan, whom we call "Papa John." John risked his life by returning to Saigon to help us safely get out of Vietnam in the nick of time. He gave me and my family the opportunity to seek freedom and prosper in the free land of the United States. This story is dedicated to John Riordan as my special thanks to him.

—XUAN NHAN

A special note of thanks goes to Mr. John P Riordan, who made our escapes and arrival in the USA possible. We never can forget his courageous-unselfish-act of going above and beyond to save all of us out of Saigon and we are forever in debt to you. We will never forget in our heart his humanity decision to return back to Saigon because simply he will not leave the team behind to suffer with the communist. I also would like to express thanks to my husband Phong who helped and contributed his memory of 40 years ago and made this story whole.

—CHRISTINE DAVIS, COI PHAM'S DAUGHTER

My grandma has asked me to write to you with her sincerest thanks and gratefulness. She will never forget what you did in risking your life to save hers, my grandpa's and many others.

I also want to add that from my perspective, I am also deeply grateful. I am not only grateful for the opportunity to have my grandparents as part of my life but I now know the whole story of how my grandparents came to the US. It has always been a blurry story as I was too young to fully grasp the details when my grandma would explain it.

I cannot express in words the true appreciation that my grandparents and entire family have for what you've given us. I hope that one day I might have the opportunity to thank you in person.

—PRISCILLA HARMON, COI PHAM'S GRANDDAUGHTER

Our "exodus" ended that day and soon our new lives in a foreign land began. Mr. Riordan continued checking up on us to ensure that our adjustment to the American way of life was going well.

Most of us are retired now. However, to us, Mr. Riordan is part of our family, our Saigon branch family. He is present in our get together. Our children all call him "Grandpa." We are all eternally indebted to him. Without his selfless efforts, God only knows what would have happened to us.

Even in their darkest hours, the people that he saved, managed to conquer adversities. In one word, Mr. Riordan's sacrifice was not in vain.

—NGUYEN THI HIEN

My husband and I are so grateful that we were rescued. We establish our family in the land of opportunity and freedom. My son is thirty years old, a successful entrepreneur and married. I am looking forward to the expansion of the future generations of my family. We are so grateful for John he is truly a hero for my entire family as well as many more families. John Riordan is the proof that one man's actions can positively affect the lives of many.

—TRUONG LE KHANH (HELEN)

As I mentioned earlier with you, you are always in our hearts.

How great a Daddy was with over a hundred kids, young and old, fled the country during that difficult ordeal.

We had prayed a lot, and our prayers had been answered. We all got out safe and sound.

We were very grateful for what you had done for us.

—LE THI MINH TAN

Love and teamwork have been our family motto. If one falls behind, the other one should help pick him up by encouraging and providing moral support. Alone one may not succeed, but 7 heads and strength put together can move mountains.

In April 1975 when the Vietcong were moving into Saigon, there was one man who gave our family this rare, once in a lifetime opportunity to live in this "land of life, liberty and justice for all" and that was the extra-ordinarily brave man, John Riordan. He made a crucial decision when [106] individuals needed him most. John had faith. John had the courage and the will to act proactively despite fear for his own life and the uncertainty of the outcome. There was one brief pivotal moment that would determine whether my family would live in fear in Vietnam or escape to a brighter future. That was when John Riordan rose above those fears and uncertainty, took a leap of faith, and risked his own life to return to Vietnam even after he'd already been safely flown out to Hong Kong. Because of John Riordan's brave choice to act positively and proactively at a critical moment in history, he literally helped saved the lives of [106] individuals from a bleak and uncertain future. Because of John Riordan's leap of faith to act positively, my family and I received the most precious gift anyone could have given us . . . the gift of a bright future together and the opportunity of living a better life. Thank you Mr. John Riordan for risking your life to save my family from the repercussions of war. We are eternally grateful for you being there for us when we were in dire need.

I could sum up everything that had happened to our family in three words: It's a MIRACLE!

—TRIEU HUYEN LANG

Year 1975 is the unforgettable year that changed my fate into a miracle new life, which I never dreamed to live in United States for my whole life. John Riordan Citibank manager (Saigon) was the one made it happened, he devoted his life into a high risk and dangerous situation to evacuate all the staffs including immediate family to get out Saigon.

—TRIEU MUOI (SYLVIA TANG)

Now, almost 40 years later, I am sure we were the lucky few being plugged from the crowd milling around looking for a way out. Our story has been told to my children and it will be told to their children that we started our new life here in America, the champion for freedom and democracy, with the help of a courageous "Dad," John Riordan and a generous FNCB, N.Y.

—PHAM THI DAN HA

John, It was like yesterday. You risked your life safety, staying behind to take us out of the country during the turmoil of the last few days of Vietnam war. We always wanted to do something to partially pay back what we owed you.

—NGUYEN THI NGOC-DUNG

ACKNOWLEDGMENTS
AND LIFE NOTES

My gratitude goes first to the members of the FNCB Saigon Branch staff and their families. There was an outpouring of encouragement among the Vietnamese when I told them I was thinking of turning our story into a book. Dozens helped me to re-create the events of nearly forty years ago by sending photos, letters, and emails and being available for questions by telephone. Their contributions to the narrative have been invaluable, and their personal stories have humbled and enlightened me in so many ways. I admire their courage and determination in overcoming adversity and succeeding in a new world. My special thanks to Cuc, Chi, Chuyen, and Minh Ha for their time and patience.

For all the following who provided written or verbal submissions of their stories, I am most appreciative: Bui Thi Bich Lien; Robert Chang; Luong Thi Mai; Nguyen Nhuoc Dam; Nguyen Thi Than; Nhan Sun Anh; Tran Thi Dau; Tran Minh Ha; Bui Tuan Tu; Dang Thi Coi; La Quoc Huy; Le Thi Anh Tuyet; Nguyen Thi Kim Oanh; Tran Thi Nga; Nguyen Thi Hien; Pham Thi Cuc; Truong Lee Khanh; Nguyen Thi Huynh Hoa; Nguyen Thi Mong Chi; Le Thi Minh Tan; Trieu Huyen Lang; Trieu Muoi; Uong Chuyen Dinh; Pham Thi Dan Ha; Uyen Dao, daughter of Dao Long Bien and Pham Thi Kim-Thoa; Minh Lee, widower of Nguyen Thi Ngoc-Dung; Catherine Do, widow, and Alex Do, son of Do Quang Quynh; Hoang Si Binh, widower of Pham Thi Dung; Hang Thu Tran, daughter of Tran Van Kien; Nguyen Nam, son of the bank's advisor Nguyen Thanh Hung;

Bill Walker, Saigon branch senior operations officer; Bob Hudspeth, first manager of FNCB Saigon; and Bob Wilcox, American resident vice president of FNCB Agana, Guam, and his staff, who greatly assisted with the greeting and temporary settlement of FNCB Vietnamese evacuees in Guam.

The evacuation and successful resettlement of the South Vietnamese in the United States was helped by a vast network of American staff of FNCB, including George Vojta, Rick Wheeler, Peter Howell, Dick Freytag, Perry Wooten, and many other loyal Citibankers. My thanks in particular to Bill Walker, Rick Roesch, and Bob Hudspeth for taking the time to talk with my writer. I owe a debt of gratitude to the memories of Michael McTighe for motivating me to go back to Saigon and Jim Eckes for getting me and all of us at FNCB Saigon safely out!

Bruce Fogel, thank you for insisting I record the facts while I could still remember them, and Chepy Valeriano, you are one of my best and most devoted friends, thank you for tireless transcription and decades of support. Jan Nicholson, you are a very treasured friend. Under Jan's wing, I was invited to many of Jan's elegant dinner parties not just in New York City, but in the Hamptons, Fire Island, and Tuscany, Italy. Jan made me tell the story of the bank's Vietnam evacuation so many times at these parties that I am sure all the repetition helped me remember it well these thirty-nine-plus years! I have so much to thank Jan for, not only her constant support of the story but her great confidence that one day it would be told in all its fullness. Last in time, but no less important in embracing this story and patiently coaching this reluctant author, are Sam Anderson, former head of the Vietnam USO and then worldwide head of the USO, and his close New York City friends artist and illustrator Sid Presberg and songwriter and game show producer Shelley Dobbins. They have been coaches to this very day, with Shelley

ninety-two now and Sam and Sid sprouting angel's wings—and on to other important business, no doubt!

I'm very fortunate that Kay and Tom Crouse have stayed in touch with me these many years. Tom was one of the two Citibank officers who ordered me to close the FNCB Saigon branch in April 1975. He's been asking about my Vietnam story ever since. Tom has been a tremendous resource to me and to my writer, Monique Brinson Demery. Thanks to the persistence of Tom and Kay, and their friend Marcus Brauchli, I got an introduction to the producers of CBS's *60 Minutes*.

The entire team at CBS News deserves my thanks and appreciation. They ran an excellent segment on my story titled "Daring Rescue Days Before the Fall of Saigon" (http://www.cbsnews.com/news /daring-rescue-days-before-the-fall-of-saigon or http://www.youtube .com/watch?v=GfdIzqS7bXE). Thank you for sharing my story with your viewers, and my gratitude to producer Shachar Bar-on, associate producer Alexandra Poolos, and the film crews in New York and Ho Chi Minh City, and Braden Bergan, who accepted and successfully completed the special assignment of locating my old Saigon villa in preparation for our Vietnam visit. My deepest thanks go to correspondent Lesley Stahl; she went above and beyond in befriending me and in providing me with invaluable advice to begin the road to publishing this book. Thanks to Lesley's daughter, Latham Taylor, for her counsel.

My agent, Amanda Urban of ICM Partners, has held my hand during this process, answering all my questions and steering this ship in calm waters. I am grateful for her guidance, along with Ron Bernstein and everyone at ICM Partners on their New York and Los Angeles staff. Thank you to Marie Arana, author, editor, journalist, and member of the Scholars Council at the Library of Congress, for being extremely generous with her time and sound advice.

Peter Osnos, founder of PublicAffairs, came highly recommended and has been a wonderful editor. His direction has brought this book to life. Peter, Clive Priddle, and the team at PublicAffairs have worked tirelessly. I want to acknowledge their great efforts to promote, distribute, and publish the book. Pete Garceau did an especially fine job on the book jacket. Thanks too to PublicAffairs' Michelle Welsh-Horst, senior project editor; Jeff Williams, book designer; and Melissa Raymond, managing editor. I would also like to thank the marketing and publicity team of Lindsay Fradkoff, Jaime Leifer, and Nicole Counts for their efforts on behalf of this book. Copyeditor Beth Wright of Trio Bookworks, proofreader Lisa Zales, indexer Robert Swanson, and cartographer Mike Morgenfeld all deserve credit for their contributions.

Thanks to Peter Osnos, I was introduced to writer and journalist Richard Pyle, who has a forty-seven-year history with the Associated Press, during three of which, in the early 1970s, he was head of the AP station office in Saigon. Richard also has a number of books to his name, one specifically about the war in Southeast Asia: *Lost Over Laos: A True Story of Tragedy, Mystery, and Friendship* (Da Capo, 2003). Richard had some immediate advice for me: "Start writing down your thoughts about your life and any memories of whatever comes to mind / vignettes." I followed Richard's advice, and I'm glad I did. Unfortunately, shortly after we got under way, Richard took seriously ill and felt the best thing for me was to get a new writer. I followed his advice, and thanks again to Peter Osnos, I was introduced to Monique Brinson Demery. I am happy to report that Richard Pyle has had successful treatment for his illness and is progressing nicely as we write.

My writer, Monique! How a beautiful young woman with two energetic children, Tommy and C.C., a very handsome and successful husband, Tom, a new home, and puppy dog, Piper, found time to work with an old farmer like me is still a mystery. Monique has been my guiding light, inspiration, artist of the English language, and North Star of my story. Additionally Monique is a very quick thinker, positive, and always ready with just the right word and answer. She has a lovely personality, great laugh, and hardy enthusiasm. Her guidance and spark have added magic to this story, and her wisdom has spun this story to its peak. If you enjoy this book, don't wait to read Monique's *Finding the Dragon Lady: The Mystery of Vietnam's Madame Nhu* (PublicAffairs, 2013).

I would be nowhere in life without my family. They taught me to have a positive, happy, humorous, and hardworking approach to life. For that I thank the memory of my great-grandparents John F. Schuetz (Chicago police officer, badge #4381, known as "Honest John" Schuetz, killed in the line of duty on the evening of January 27, 1919) and Catherine Schuetz; my grandparents William Francis Riordan and Jane Elizabeth Broadwell Riordan, and Bartholomew Murphy and Rose Schuetz Murphy; as well as my parents, William Joseph Riordan and Rosemary Murphy Riordan. To my brother, William Bartholomew Riordan, and his wife, Kathleen, and to my sister, Rosemary Riordan Palicki, and her husband, Leonard, thank you for being my greatest friends and for raising such wonderful families yourselves. My nieces and nephews are terrific. I recognize that I have big shoes to fill as an uncle—my own were sparkling stars of Chicago and pretty fantastic, not to be outdone by my aunts: Great Uncle Henry Schuetz and Great Uncle Harold Burns and his wife, Great Aunt Clara; Great Aunt Nell Murphy Duffy and her daughter, "Aunt" Cele Duffy; John B. Murphy, C.M., and Clarence "Slug" Murphy, both missionary priests in China; George Murphy and his wife, Dorothy Karasinski Murphy. From my father's Kansas City side of the family Ferg and Ruth Ferguson; uncles James Riordan and John Clement Riordan; Margaret Broadwell Riordan and George

Riordan. Add to these relatives our adopted family of relatives, the Ostranders: "Old" Joe, Maggie, "Aunt Helen," Dorothy, and Joel and his family. The Ostranders took my dad in in the Depression and helped him get a good job and were instrumental in introducing my dad to my mom. Each and every one of these personalities, relatives and adopted relatives, had stories to tell and told many different and exciting versions of them.

I honor the memory of my neighbor growing up in Chicago, Dan Cullen, who called me his "No. 1 man." I was always interested in the home projects he was undertaking. Mr. Cullen encouraged me to help, learn, and enjoy working with my hands. He died a tragic but heroic death on December 7, 1957. The Chicago El motorman was operating one of the old wooden Elevated 4 coach trains in morning rush hour. It caught on fire just as the train arrived at the Howard El Station, but instead of stopping the train at the station, Mr. Cullen drove it through to avoid harming the crowd of passengers on the platform. He stopped the train beyond the station, where he was unable to exit. To save so many, he burned to death.

Bert Finzer was a neighbor lad and good friend my age who died on a mission in the Vietnam War as a US Air Force pilot.

My work ethic has served me well in life, and for that I'm greatly appreciative of the formative experiences I was given. My first job was given to me by Charlie and Jim Wilson when they employed me for one dollar an hour at the Wilson Candy Factory. Bob Wells and other Junior Achievement advisors from the Chicago office of Ernst and Ernst (now known as Ernst and Young) advised my brother and me on making and selling door to door aluminum "potato baker makers" and later "western-style carry-all trays." The principal at St. Margaret Mary's grade school in Chicago, Sister Mary Liguori, and the nuns participated in a project called "Let's move this hopeless case along!" At Gordon Tech High School in Chicago, Father Gracz, the principal, was one of my angels. I have family friend Tom Cotter to thank for strongly encouraging me to go to college, and at St. Joseph College Rensselaer, Indiana, there were also several professors who nudged this lad along. Special acknowledgment to Professors Ralph A. Marini, Robert W. Morell, and Father Edward P. McCarthy. Their help got me accepted to an MBA program at Roosevelt University in Chicago, but I didn't avoid a few speed bumps, like the F in finance (of all subjects!). However, thanks to Dean Brandel L. Works, I was given one more chance, and true to his name, that worked.

There were so many helpful Citibank officers and staff in New York City, Japan, and the Philippines who helped me in my career before my assignment to Vietnam. Just a few I'd like to name here who didn't figure into the Saigon story: Kay Yoshida, the Japan desk officer in New York; Funaki-san, the "stencho" (manager of the Osaka branch); Kawanishi-san, the operations manager of the Osaka branch; Ase-san, secretary to the Osaka branch manager; and Takano Masako, secretary to Japan country head George Vojta. I knew Nam Lee Yick from FNCB in New York. He taught me the "Asian Rule of Ten," which came to mean, at least for me, that you need not worry about the details when calculating, just round everything to the nearest large number and leave it to the number guys in the back rooms of the bank to get the details right. I always felt that I was more of a salesman than a "real" banker!

In June 1982, I was making more money from my real estate investments and rental income than I was as a vice president (one of a thousand) at Citibank. I felt that the bank was changing, becoming less client-relationship-oriented and more "cold nose" driven. Also at that time I was beginning to lose friends from the AIDS epidemic, and I was forty years old. I thought I'd like to pursue my real estate business of brownstones and brokerage at my pace, and have time for myself and my family and friends who needed help.

In 1989 my parents called me from Chicago. They had decided to sell our family house and move to a rental apartment; they were finding it increasingly difficult just to keep up home ownership. Their retirement dream, and mine, was to own a farm in Wisconsin. They asked, "Would you move out from New York and buy a farm with us and build a house and live there with us?" I said yes! And so in the summer of 1991 we closed on our beautiful 41.55-acre farm with a 13-acre hardwood lot. The property overlooks Lake Michigan. From that time we started planning our house and hoped to start building in early 1993. As fate would have it, in mid-October 1992 my dad suffered a large intracranial hemorrhage and died in early November. After resting for a year or so and rethinking, my mother and I broke ground in March 1995, and moved in October. I named the property after my parents, William and Rosemary, and it became Willrose Farm. My mother enjoyed seven years of good health here, right up to her death on December 16, 2002. Molly, our yellow Lab, kept me company until time took her on April 27, 2009.

Then I met Gilbert. Without him in my life and his organization, knowledge of computing, and teaching skills, and most of all his love, I would be writing all of this with a quill pen on parchment paper and be years behind. Gilbert's mother spoke nothing but Cantonese, and I learned maybe five words of the language. Nevertheless, love shines through, and I always felt loved and embraced in her presence and with her generous acceptance of my love of her precious son.

There are so many other people in my life who have been and remain dear and supportive friends. Maybe if I am allowed a second book, I can spin the yarns each has inspired in me. For now, dear friends, please accept my gratitude for your gift of friendship: Dr. Chester and Loretta Stanley; Frank and Gwen McAuliffe; Eddie

Gregoire; Sarah Sundvahl; Buck and Grace Kane; Bill Metzler; Bob Hiett; Nora O'Malley; Joan Nolan Finnerty; Andy Fantacci; the staff of The R&D Command, Office of the Army Surgeon General, in particular General Colin F. Vorder Bruegge, Majors Byron Howlett, JR, and Jack Webb, Col. Crosby, and Nathan Price; my two immediate Vietnam bosses in the joint command Studies and Operations Group (SOG), Navy Lt./Dr. Bob Ramuzzi and Navy Lt./Dr. Rudy Gross, and our Vietnamese counterpart Dr. (Bacci) Tri; Emer Manawis; Kathleen Dollymore; Mary McDonough; Dr. (Bacci) Thach; Eiji Tachibana; Kumiyoshi Asikaga; Stephen Racaza; Clem and Gerry Bichler; Jack Murdoch; Nguyen Hai Viet; Clarence Wasson; Craig Southwood Palmer; Bill Chen, my Chinese language teacher and friend to this day; Bruce Brenn; Carl Desch; Backson Liu; Jim Weadock; Milly and David Fulton; Dan Montana; Wesley Sutliff; Dr. John Young; George Snyder; Harsa Oseman; Jack Byers; Eddie Buxbaum; Bob Newman; Peter Morales and Jim Mancato; Harry Pangburn; Dallas Pratt; Andrew Pan; Peter Frankel; Joe Brown; George Grau; Herb Rogers, S.J.; Billy McNichols, S.J.; Mary Guthrie Riordan; Mary Ellen (Murphy) and Tim Hughes; Killian Burton; Peter and Margaret Poull; Otto Finger, artist and friend; Al and Barbara Weyker; Bill Karrels; Dan Lagerman; John Locke; John Schoenknech and the rest of the Milwaukee FrontRunners/Walkers; Lynde Uihlein; Arturo Ysmael, S.D.S.; Hariett (The Spy!) Cavanaugh Arnold; Edith Bahringer, Jerry Shoemaker, and all my swimming pool pals; and my Thursday night Wine-and-Cheese friends, especially Barbara Frenz and Jill Kunsmann, who brainstormed book titles with me.

And to all the unnamed kind and gentle souls who were good to me in countless ways along the journey thus far, my respect and gratitude.

JOHN P. RIORDAN
Willrose Farm, Belgium, Wisconsin

NOTES

CHAPTER 2   APRIL 3, SAIGON: THE CALL

1. Paul Vogle, "Troops Beat Out Civilians in Rush for Da Nang Plane," *New York Times*, March 29, 1975.

2. Michael Manning, "The Interview: Pan Am's Al Topping and Last Flight Out," Michael Manning.tv, August 1, 2006, http://michaelmanninginterview .blogspot.com/2006/08/last-flight-out-exclusive-interview.html.

CHAPTER 3   THE IDES OF MARCH, 1975

1. John Riordan, telex to FNCB Hong Kong, March 26, 1975.

2. Phillip L. Zweig, *Wriston: Walter Wriston, Citibank and the Rise and Fall of American Financial Supremacy* (New York: Crown, 1995), 166.

CHAPTER 4   APRIL 3, DISASTER PREPAREDNESS

1. Stephen Daggett, "Costs of Major U.S. Wars: Congressional Research Service Report for Congress (RS22926)," Navy Department Library, July 24, 2008, http://www.history.navy.mil/library/online/costs_of_major_us_wars.htm.

2. "Statistical Information about Fatal Casualties of the Vietnam War: Electronic Records Reference Report," National Archives, April 29, 2008, www.archives.gov/research/military/vietnam-war/casualty-statistics.html.

3. William S. Turley, *The Second Indochina War* (Boulder: Westview, 1986), 195–197; Charles Hirschman, Samuel Preston, and Vu Manh Loi, "Vietnamese Casualties During the American War: A New Estimate," *Population and Development Review* 21, no. 4 (December 1995): 783–812, https://csde.washington .edu/~glynn/c/pubs/VietnameseCasualtiesDuringAmerican.pdf.

4. "Nixon, Kissinger, and the 'Decent Interval'" (audio recording and transcript), August 3, 1972, Miller Center, University of Virginia, http://millercenter .org/presidentialclassroom/exhibits/nixon-kissinger-and-the-decent-interval.

5. Information about the Paris Peace Accords and Nixon's promise to South Vietnamese president Thieu and Le Duan's determination from A. J. Langguth, *Our Vietnam: The War, 1954–1975* (New York: Simon & Schuster, 2000), 696–698, 703, 706.

6. Linda Greenhouse, "Justices to Hear Citibank-Cuba Case," *New York Times*, October 19, 1982.

7. Details of the Japanese camp in Philippines, the Chinese Revolution, and Wriston's responses are from Peter Starr, *Citibank: A Century in Asia* (Singapore: Editions Didier Millet, 2002), 74–75, 80, 83–84.

CHAPTER 5 APRIL 3, MONEY ON FIRE

1. David Butler, *The Fall of Saigon: Scenes from the Sudden End of a Long War* (New York: Simon & Schuster, 1985), 144.

2. A. J. Langguth, *Our Vietnam: The War, 1954–1975* (New York: Simon & Schuster, 2000), 710, 717.

3. Butler, *The Fall of Saigon*, 150.

4. Ibid., 64.

5. Ibid., 149.

6. George J. Veith, *Black April: The Fall of South Vietnam, 1973–1975* (New York: Encounter Books, 2012), 122.

CHAPTER 6 APRIL 4, LEAVING SAIGON

1. "People & Events: Operation Babylift (1975)," *American Experience*, PBS, http://www.pbs.org/wgbh/amex/daughter/peopleevents/e_babylift.html.

2. Ibid.

3. James Barron, "Edward Daly Dies; Airline Chairman," Obituaries, *New York Times*, January 24, 1984.

4. Charles Patterson's recollections quoted from LDE, "Charlie Patterson's Vietnam," Pushing On (blog), December 16, 2012, http://lde421.blogspot .com/2012/12/charlie-pattersons-vietnam.html.

CHAPTER 7 APRIL 5–12, HONG KONG

1. "Hong Kong Hilton, Largest in the East," *Montreal Gazette*, June 1, 1963, 9.

2. LDE, "On Borrowed Time: Brian Ellis Remembers the Fall of Phnom Penh," Pushing On (blog), June 10, 2014, http://lde421.blogspot.com/2014/06/on -borrowed-time-brian-ellis-remembers.html; Mark Phillip Yablonka, *Distant War: Recollections of Vietnam, Laos and Cambodia* (Bennington, VT: Merriam, 2009), Kindle edition; interview with Jim Eckes, New York City, 1990.

CHAPTER 8 APRIL 14, SAIGON BRIEFINGS

1. Peter Starr, *Citibank: A Century in Asia* (Singapore: Editions Didier Millet, 2002), 57.

2. LDE, "Wolf Lehmann's Vietnam," Pushing On (blog), December 15, 2012, http://lde421.blogspot.com/2012/12/wolf-lehmanns-vietnam.html.

3. Interview with Wolfgang J. Lehmann by Robert Martens, Association for Diplomatic Studies and Training, Foreign Affairs Oral History Project, May 9, 1989, http://lcweb2.loc.gov/service/mss/mfdip/2005%20txt%20files/2004leh03.txt.

4. Interview with Fred Charles Thomas Jr. by Charles Stuart Kennedy, Association for Diplomatic Studies and Training, Foreign Affairs Oral History Project, March 8, 1995, http://www.adst.org/OH%20TOCs/THOMAS,%20Fred%20Charles%20Jr.toc.pdf.

CHAPTER 9 APRIL 17, DINNER IN HONG KONG

1. "WSAG" was the Washington Special Actions Group, a small interdepartmental group of high-level decision makers chaired by Kissinger.

2. "Telegram for Ambassador Graham Martin Concerning Interagency Review of State of Play in South Vietnam," April 18, 1975, National Archives, http://docsteach.org/documents/7367440/detail?menu=closed&mode=search&sortBy=relevance&q=kissinger%2C+martin%2C+&commit=Go.

CHAPTER 10 APRIL 18, RETURN TO SAIGON

1. Daniel L. Haulman, "Vietnam Evacuation: Operation Frequent Wind," Air Force Historical Studies Office, n.d., http://www.afhso.af.mil/shared/media/document/AFD-120823-033.pdf.

CHAPTER 12 APRIL 21, BREAKING CURFEW, SAIGON

1. Fox Butterfield, "Nguyen Van Thieu Is Dead at 76: Last President of South Vietnam," *New York Times*, October 1, 2001; "1975: Vietnam's President Thieu Resigns," On This Day: 21 April, BBC, http://news.bbc.co.uk/onthisday/hi/dates/stories/april/21/newsid_2935000/2935347.stm; David Butler, *The Fall of Saigon: Scenes from the Sudden End of a Long War* (New York: Simon & Schuster, 1985), 293; "Nguyen Van Thieu," Obituaries, *Telegraph* (London), October 1, 2001, http://www.telegraph.co.uk/news/obituaries/1358069/Nguyen-Van-Thieu.html.

NOTES

CHAPTER 13 APRIL 22, DAY ONE

1. Daniel L. Haulman, "Vietnam Evacuation: Operation Frequent Wind," Air Force Historical Studies Office, n.d., http://www.afhso.af.mil/shared/media/document/AFD-120823–033.pdf.
2. David Butler, *The Fall of Saigon: Scenes from the Sudden End of a Long War* (New York: Simon & Schuster, 1985), 278.
3. Ibid., 279.
4. Ibid., 280.

CHAPTER 14 APRIL 23–24, DAYS TWO AND THREE

1. Carl Posey, "50 Years of Hercules," *Air & Space Magazine* (September 2004), http://www.airspacemag.com/history-of-flight/50-years-of-hercules-5504946/?all.
2. Daniel L. Haulman, "Vietnam Evacuation: Operation Frequent Wind," Air Force Historical Studies Office, n.d., http://www.afhso.af.mil/shared/media/document/AFD-120823-033.pdf.
3. David Butler, *The Fall of Saigon: Scenes from the Sudden End of a Long War* (New York: Simon & Schuster, 1985), 322.

CHAPTER 15 APRIL 25, DAY FOUR

1. Jessica J. Savage, "After the Fall," *Desert Exposure* (April 2005), http://www.desertexposure.com/200504/200504_saigon.html.
2. Ibid., and J. Edward Lee and H. C. "Toby" Haynsworth, *Nixon, Ford, and the Abandonment of South Vietnam* (Jefferson, NC: McFarland, 2002), 135.
3. A. J. Langguth, *Our Vietnam: The War, 1954–1975* (New York: Simon & Schuster, 2000), 721.

CHAPTER 16 APRIL 26, FLYING OUT

1. "Chuck Neil's Vietnam: Dreaming of a White Christmas," Pushing On (blog), December 14, 2012, http://lde421.blogspot.com/2012/12/chuck-neils-vietnam-dreaming-of-white.html; Larry Engelmann, *Tears Before the Rain: An Oral History of the Fall of South Vietnam* (New York: Da Capo, 1997), 194.
2. A. J. Langguth, *Our Vietnam: The War, 1954–1975* (New York: Simon & Schuster, 2000), 724.

3. Dan E. Feltham, *When Big Blue Went to War: A History of the IBM Corporation's Mission in Southeast Asia during the Vietnam War (1965–1975)* (Bloomington, IN: Abbott, 2012).

4. Langguth, *Our Vietnam*, 727.

5. Details of the final chaos in Saigon are from George Esper, "Evacuation from Saigon Tumultuous at the End," *New York Times International*, April 30, 1975; ibid., 727–729; Frank Snepp, "Decent Interval: An Insider's Account of Saigon's Indecent End," n.d., http://franksnepp.com/decent-interval; Daniel L. Haulman, "Vietnam Evacuation: Operation Frequent Wind," Air Force Historical Studies Office, n.d., http://www.afhso.af.mil/shared/media/document/AFD -120823-033.pdf.

EPILOGUE

1. Alicia Campi, "From Refugees to Americans: Thirty Years of Vietnamese Immigration to the United States," *Immigration Daily*, 2006, http://www.ilw .com/articles/2006,0313-campi.shtm#_5.

2. Statement by Secretary of State Cyrus Vance before the Sub-Committee on Immigration, Refugees, and International Law of the House Judiciary Committee, July 31, 1979.

3. Samantha Marshall, "Man Who Fled Saigon Leads Citibank Back," *Asian Wall Street Journal*, February 23, 1998, 12.

INDEX

INDEX

John P. Riordan is a former vice president of Citibank. After receiving his MBA from Roosevelt University in Chicago, Riordan joined the US Army Medical Service Corps, landing in Vietnam at the end of the 1968 Tet Offensive, where he was assigned to a clandestine unit, the Studies and Observations Group. Riordan went on to a banking career and spent more than a decade working with Citibank with a focus on the bank's branches in East Asia. Riordan left the banking world in 1982 to focus on real estate investments, and he now owns and runs an environmental farm in Wisconsin next to some really big buffalo.

Monique Brinson Demery took her first trip to Vietnam in 1997 as part of a study abroad program with Hobart and William Smith Colleges. She was the recipient of a US Department of Education grant to attend the Vietnamese Advanced Summer Institute in Hanoi, and in 2003 she received a master's degree in East Asia regional studies from Harvard University. Demery's first book, *Finding the Dragon Lady: The Mystery of Vietnam's Madame Nhu*, was published in 2013. Demery lives in Chicago.

PublicAffairs is a publishing house founded in 1997. It is a tribute to the standards, values, and flair of three persons who have served as mentors to countless reporters, writers, editors, and book people of all kinds, including me.

I. F. STONE, proprietor of *I. F. Stone's Weekly*, combined a commitment to the First Amendment with entrepreneurial zeal and reporting skill and became one of the great independent journalists in American history. At the age of eighty, Izzy published *The Trial of Socrates*, which was a national bestseller. He wrote the book after he taught himself ancient Greek.

BENJAMIN C. BRADLEE was for nearly thirty years the charismatic editorial leader of *The Washington Post*. It was Ben who gave the *Post* the range and courage to pursue such historic issues as Watergate. He supported his reporters with a tenacity that made them fearless and it is no accident that so many became authors of influential, best-selling books.

ROBERT L. BERNSTEIN, the chief executive of Random House for more than a quarter century, guided one of the nation's premier publishing houses. Bob was personally responsible for many books of political dissent and argument that challenged tyranny around the globe. He is also the founder and longtime chair of Human Rights Watch, one of the most respected human rights organizations in the world.

.   .   .

For fifty years, the banner of Public Affairs Press was carried by its owner Morris B. Schnapper, who published Gandhi, Nasser, Toynbee, Truman, and about 1,500 other authors. In 1983, Schnapper was described by *The Washington Post* as "a redoubtable gadfly." His legacy will endure in the books to come.

Peter Osnos, *Founder and Editor-at-Large*